IT'S ME AGAIN, LORD

Jack McArdle ss cc

It's me again, Lord

Heart-to-heart chats between God and myself

the columba press

First published in 1998 by
the columba press
55A Spruce Avenue, Stillorgan Industrial Park,
Blackrock, Co Dublin

Cover by Bill Bolger
Cover photo by Marie McDonald
Origination by The Columba Press
Printed in Ireland by Genprint Ltd, Dublin

ISBN 185607 242 8

Contents

Introduction

This is not a prayer-book in the normal understanding of that concept. It is a book of prayers, of course, but I hope it will prove to be much more than that. I wouldn't dare tell others what words they should use, how they should speak to God, how they should relate to God. The inspiration and the generation of all this comes from God himself, through the presence and work of his Spirit in our hearts.

Prayer has had many definitions over the years, and we are now approaching the possibility of accepting the simple fact that defining exactly what prayer is, is something beyond our grasp. Communication is at least two-way, or not at all. Prayer is both listening to and speaking to God, and words are not an essential part of either. When I decide to use words, I don't have to choose words. Coming before God is like opening out the full canvas of my life in his presence. When Adam and Eve sinned, we are told that they hid because they were afraid. The road back to the Garden involves coming out of hiding, into the truth, and into the freedom that truth brings.

In this book I have prayed for the guidance of the Spirit, reached down into my heart, and written the words that came from there. I know very well that only those who are depressed, bereaved, lonely, or afraid, are qualified to put words on how they feel. I have stepped out in faith in trying to capture some of those feelings, and I trust the good Lord and the understanding of the reader, to fill in the many gaps that must surely be there. These prayers are intended to help, and they can help best if used in the most helpful way. For example, it is possible that only one or two prayers speak directly to the situation in which a particular person lives. It would not surprise me, indeed, if at some later date these prayers appeared on separate leaflets. I will give that some thought in the not-too-distant future.

Of necessity, there is a certain level of artificiality about these prayers, in that each is divided into two separate monologues. I am very conscious of this, but I am also hopeful that, when used for the umpteenth time, as I speak I will also hear God's response at the very same time. What is offered here is nothing more than a kick-start on a journey, and I have helped you only when you don't need the words in this book to open your heart of God, or to get to know the heart of God.

The final chapters are much more than just 'fillers'. A life without reflection is not worth living. What I offer is intended to stir up reflection, to give food for thought, and to supply the spiritual chewing-gum for the day. The idle mind is the devil's workshop, and the inner spirit can be a Third World, right within my own heart. It is important to become familiar with God. By that, I don't mean to know all about him or to have some inside track to his attention. I mean being aware of his presence, and being at ease in his presence.

One serious question for you now: What image of God do you work out of? If you have an Irish Catholic male God, you are sure to have problems with the relationship, because he will be watching you all the time, you will do everything within your power to keep him happy, you will be burdened with guilt, and after all that you'll be terrified to die! There is only one God, and Jesus told us to call him Abba, Daddy, Father.

Prayer before all prayers

It is suggested that you might develop the habit of saying these, or similar prayers, at the very beginning of all your prayer-times.

Holy Spirit, breath and power of God, please be in my heart now, as a Spirit of Truth, so that I may be sincere and genuine in what I am about. I know that I can say prayers, but I certainly cannot pray. Prayer is something sacred, because it brings me face to face with the Almighty God, and, therefore, it is something that only you can do through me, with me, and for me. Please be in my words to turn them into prayer. I trust you in my heart, so that I can pour out my heart and be sure that I am in the presence of God.

Mary, my Mother, caretaker of my heart, please continue to supervise the miracle of Incarnation within. You did in a perfect way what I'm struggling towards. Your basic prayer was YES, and everything that happened after that was the work of God. Please continue to pray in me, with me, and for me. Go to Jesus on my behalf again and again, so that my heart may become a prayer room, a Pentecost place, a place of the Spirit, an Upper Room. Thank you for being with me; it makes all the difference in the world. Please teach me to pray with a grateful heart. Thank you.

1. With my heavenly Father

Listen...

My dear dear child, you whom I have loved from the very beginning. It was in total love you were created, just as it is my wish that all my children might be pro-created in love. I am love. I have no other way of being and of acting. Love is restless until it receives some response. Love is always giving, always reaching out, always hoping. I think of you all the time, because if I ceased to think of you, you would no longer exist. Creating you, and continuing to create you, is my gift to you. I didn't create you as some whim of fancy, just to please myself. Because I am love, I created you so that I could share that love with you. I am the source of all life, and so I created you because I chose to share the gift of life with you. It was you, and you only, I was thinking of when I created you, and when I decided that you should share life and love with me. Creating you was but the beginning of a journey. I didn't create you to let you float aimlessly in space until something happened to end the journey. When I created you, I set you on a journey, on a path, which I had marked out for you. My love hovers over you as you travel, even when you are completely unaware of this, or you don't care to know. My word is sacred, my promises are eternal, and when I begin something I take full responsibility until that creation is completed, until it becomes what I had created it to be. I know it is not possible for you, by yourself, to understand or to grasp the scope of my love for you. That is why I sent my Son Jesus. He came to teach you about my love. He came to tell you that I love you. He even told you that I love you as much as I love

10

him. Because he came to do my will, he never said anything unless I told him to. I told him to tell you about the forgiving Father in the story of the Prodigal Son; about how I care for the birds of the air and the lilies of the field; about how much I want you to come back to the Garden.

You are very special to me. It certainly is not my will that any one of you should be lost. All I ask is that you respond to my love. I would never ever force or compel a response from you. There are no conditions to my love, and all I ask is that you accept my love. I really want you to live in reality, to live with conviction, to live life fully. I want you to accept the complete parcel, the complete gift of life, and not to settle for some form of existence. That was never my intention in creating you. I want you, in yourself, to reflect something of the reality that I am. I want you to live with a sense of destiny, and with horizons of eternity. I fully appreciate how difficult it is for a finite human mind to even slightly grasp the concept of unlimited unconditional love. It is important, therefore, that you understand that this is your ultimate goal, the direction in which I lead you, and not something you can fully understand right now. In fact, during this earthly part of your journey you have enough to go on with! When you accept my love, you become one with me, you become united with me, because I am love; when you live in love, you live in me, and I live in you. My Son Jesus came to do my will. All I ask is that you make your will available to me, that you have the goodwill to be open to me. Goodwill is like a switch and, when I touch it, it switches on the machine. Have you ever watched someone struggling with a car or a motor-lawnmower, trying to get it started? On the other hand, you are very familiar with a switch that fulfils its function once you touch it. That might help you understand the idea of goodwill. The switch doesn't generate or supply the power; it simply makes the connection, and allows the power to flow. You are familiar with switches that are operated by remote control. These controls activate something else, and things begin to happen. I never ask you for will-power; all I ask is that you have the will, and I will supply the power. I ask for openness of heart, of mind, of spirit, and I will do the rest. There is nothing impossible to me. I know you have a big heart, and a good heart. I know that you fail because you are weak, not because you are evil. Because I understand you so well, I am never involved in condemnation or in rejection. How you think of me is very very important. I want you to examine very carefully the image you have in your mind when you think of me. If you think of me as some sort of eagle-eye in the sky, watching your every move, taking note of every failure, and someone who is going to extract the final penny, then you have entirely missed the whole point of the gospel, and every word that my Son Jesus told you.

Because I have given you free-will, you often get in the way of my plans for you. You often forget who and what you are, and that I am God, and not you! There are so many times when I wish you would let me take over, and do for you all those things you never could do for yourself. Quite often this is prompted by your own goodwill, and your determination to be good. The problem arises when your efforts at being good are limited to your own human efforts, and I am not involved. Is it not a fact that you sometimes only come back to me when you have failed? I smile again when I think of this, because I am a Parent, a Father/Mother, and what parent is not all too familiar with the child running in from the street with a cut knee, or a bleeding finger? Seeing me, and thinking of me as a parent, and thinking of our relationship as one of parent/child is something that should help you a great deal in your conscious awareness of me.

My plans for you never change. I created you in love, to love, and to become love. That plan and purpose is always there, and it never changes. You, however, can put yourself outside of my plans, through the way you choose to do things, and how you choose to have things. I can do nothing about that, because I will never ever interfere in the gift of free-will I gave you. A decision is not real unless it is freely made. Love is a decision. I cannot give you anything unless you choose to accept it. I always offer you choices, because you are free to make choices. You can choose how your life should be, both now, and for eternity. You have a choice between life and death. I always ask you to choose life. Life as you know it now is nothing compared to the fullness of life that lies up ahead for you. The fact is, however, that that fullness of life begins now, it develops now, it evolves now, and all that is life now is but a foreshadowing of what is to come. In the Garden, your first parents chose another way of living, another way of being. I sent my Son Jesus to redeem that situation, and restore you to the original happiness I had intended for all my children. Jesus came to offer you life in abundance. I continually invite you to choose life, to choose that life in abundance. I always await your response at every step of the journey of life.

I know you through and through. At every moment I am fully aware of everything you do, and everything you think. I am fully aware of how you feel, and of what you fear. I want to be part of all that, and I am always hoping that you will let me be part of everything. Because you are a very precious part of my creation, I take full responsibility for all that is best for you. With my gift of life comes all that is needed to live that life to the full. I supply the manna, the daily bread, for every day I give you. Life is a package, to use a word you will understand. With the gift of life comes whatever it takes to live that life. Your life is totally unique, because you are totally unique. When I created you I broke up the mould, and there never has been, nor will there ever be another person exactly like you. Even your fingerprint is uniquely yours, just as is the composition of your blood. It is very important that you understand and accept this fact. You have gifts that are unique to you. Even if you were born deaf, or unable to walk, you have all it takes to live life fully, as I intend it for you. I never ask anyone to be anyone else, or to live like anyone else. Every human being on this earth comes with an equal right to live here, even if other people deprive them of that basic right. Just as I would never force you to do the good, so I never stop others from doing the evil. Free-will is a two-edged sword that can work for good or for evil. Just as you have choices, and can make choices, so it is with humanity as a whole. I will never interfere directly, because that would be to deprive one group of their free-will, and to prevent the good people from doing what it takes to oppose and over-come the evil. While I will not interfere directly, I will certainly give what it takes to those of goodwill, so they can be my in-struments for overcoming the evil. You have within you, as part of your new redeemed creation, all that it takes to over-come all evil. Because my Spirit lives in you, he needs your hands, feet, and voice to do the good, and to speak the good. If you supply the will, the availability, I will do everything else.

I always wish you well. I always want what is best for you. When you thwart my plans for you, when your self-will runs riot, and when your selfishness makes you deaf or heed-less to the voice of conscience; at all such times, I just continue to love you, and to want everything that is for your good. I al-ways hope; I always and ever hope that you will listen, that you will heed, that you will respond. It is never too late for me. The only 'yes' I care about is the one you whisper just now. My whole relationship with you is based on the on-going gift of being able to begin again. A mother watches her child take those first very cautious steps. There will be many falls before the child is able to walk unaided, and with confi-dence. The mother sees every improvement, rather than tak-ing note of every fall. I see you as my child, and I watch you every day. I see your attempts to live as I would wish you, and I see the failures and the falls. You fail because you are weak, not because you are evil. My total attention is directed to you right now. The very fact that you are listening to my words now is all that I ask right now. Thank you for being with me, and for listening. I ask for no return for the gift of life I have given you, beyond the great joy it gives me to live that life with you, and to see your goodwill, and your attempts to live that life. When you live in love, you live in me, and I am living in you. Your goodwill is the material that produces that love.

Speak…
Heavenly Father, Holy and all-powerful God, thank you for allowing me come to you, and speak to you. After Moses spoke to you and heard you speak, the people saw that his face was radiant with light. He had stood face to face before the All-holy God. Father, I come before you with very simple credentials. You are my Father, I am your child. I come before you now, knowing I am always before you, even when I am not aware of that fact. I open out my heart, my hands, my whole being to you. I know that I cannot hide from your gaze, and I have no desire to do so. I want to open out the canvas of my life before you … out … out … out to the very edges. There are parts of it that don't make a pretty sight; there are parts that are not very life-giving; there are parts that are not very alive. I trust your gaze of love and total acceptance because, unless I was sure of that, I wouldn't dare stand before you. I know and accept that you love me exactly as I am. However, I'm more grateful still that you love me much much more than that; and therefore, that you won't leave me the way I am. Father, I have no desire to be anything other than what you want me to be. I stand before you now with all that I am, the good, the bad, the ugly. I'm not looking for any commendation, or expecting any condemnation. It's just me as I am, it's me as you see me. Abba, Daddy, Father, I know that you can read and hear my heart. I cannot ever hope to put in words all I want to say, whether that be asking for forgiveness or giving you thanks. The only anchor I can cling to is the honest desire within my heart to be open to you, and to become everything to which you call me. I know

well that I cannot trust myself, because my experience gives
me no good reason to do so. I also know that I am happiest
when I am aware of you and your presence. I know, of course,
that it would be impossible, and would not be expected by
you, that I should be aware of you and of your presence always. I cling to the image of parent and child, where there is a
very special love, but they are not always with each other, or
thinking of each other. You are God, and you alone in the
whole universe are capable of having me in your mind and
vision at all times.

I remember, earlier in life, how I set out to gain your approval and your commendation. I was determined to be perfect in your sight, and always be pleasing to you. I smile now
when I think of that, and somehow I believe that you smile
too. I know now that I had it all wrong, but the goodwill was
there and, so, I could never wander too far away from you as
long as that was so, no matter how crazy my ideas were, or
how unrealistic my dreams. I now know that you were with
me at every step of the way, even when I chose to walk alone,
as if that could be. When I look back down the corridor of
time, the one thing that strikes me most is your extraordinary
patience. You stuck with me through thick and thin; whenever
I turned back to you, you were always there for me. At some
of those times I turned to you because everyone else, including myself, seemed to turn away from me. I turned to you
when I came in touch with my frailty, either in matters of
worry, of health, or confusion. I believe what Jesus tells me
about the Forgiving Father in the story of the Prodigal Son,
and I know that you are the Father, and that I am the prodigal
child. There are many times, indeed, when you see me as the
self-righteous brother, in the way I think of or treat those who
are different from me. I would dearly love to be like the forgiving father towards others. All I can do, again and again, is
offer you my goodwill, and my genuine desire to become all
you created me to be. You created me in love, and for love,
and I believe that my best response, in love, is to constantly

desire that your will for me be brought to its completion, and that my own self-will does not get in the way. As it happens, Father, I don't like flying, and when I'm up there in the sky, I am a little more conscious of you being in control! I try to bring that awareness back to earth with me, and remind myself again and again that you are at the controls, even when you allow me to be co-pilot from time to time! It frightens me to think of Jesus feeling absolutely alone on the Cross. I know you were still there with him, but the feeling of being totally alone must be one of the worst experiences possible to the human heart.

I never think of you creating me and then just leaving me to my own devices, to my own whim and fancy. I just have to believe that your creation of me is on-going; that I am now in the womb of Divinity, being formed in the image of your Son, Jesus. Father, to be honest with you, I have to believe that this is how you see it, and that you know what is happening, or how it's happening. From my point of view, from my perspective, I could easily get discouraged, because it's difficult to see any improvement. While admitting that I'm not as good as I ought to be,. I thank you, though, that there are times when I believe that I'm a bit better than I used to be! I rely totally on your love to see me through. All I can do is hang in there, and believe that you know what you're doing. There are times today when, with developments and events in both church and state, I'm not sure what's happening. It's at such times that I turn to you afresh, and turn my concerns over to you. I know then that they are in safe hands. I don't need to know the why of everything, and I don't want to know it. All I want to know is that my goodwill is pleasing to you, that I live in conscious awareness of you, and that I make myself available to you. I know you would never ask me, nor expect me, to do the impossible; and what you do ask, I can rely on you to give me the grace to respond and to obey. Abba, Daddy, Father, thank you, thank you for being there, and being there for me always.

2. With Jesus, my Lord and Saviour

Listen…

My friend, yes, I call you my friend… You are my friend, because I came to be your friend. The religious leaders condemned me because of my friends! You didn't choose me; no, I have chosen you. I have called you by name, you are mine. You are very precious to me, you are precious in my eyes. If you were lost, I would leave the ninety-nine, and go to find you, and bring you back, so that where I am you also may be. I want you to be with me, and I want to be with you. I want to live in you, so that I can continue my work through you. I want to speak, to touch, and to listen through your senses. I walked this world like you do now. I had a mission entrusted to me by my Father. When I had completed the first part of that mission, I returned to my Father and, through the power of my Spirit, I entrust the second part to you. That's how important I think you are. I spoke of a farmer who sowed good wheat in his field and, when the wheat appeared, there were many weeds there also. The wheat is the good work of my Father's creation. After creating something 'He saw that it was good'. The weeds of sin, sickness and death were not part of my Father's creation, but were planted by Satan, the father of lies. I came to destroy those weeds, wither them at the root, as it were. All I ask now is that you accept that fact, live with the knowledge of that victory, and pass on that Good News to others. I don't ask you to save anyone! All I ask is that you personally come to experience my salvation in your own life and, as a result, you can witness to that salvation for the sake of others. I never want you to speak to others about being saved, or about how to be saved, until you your-self have personally experienced my salvation in your own life. I need you, because you are essential to the completion of my plan of salvation.

I know you through and through. I do not condemn you, because that is not why I came. I came to take on human na-ture, with all of its brokenness, so that I could undo the harm that sin effected, and make all things new again. When I took on human nature, I took on yours, and it is very important to me that you believe and always remember that. The greatest sin in this world is the fact that so many don't believe me, or believe in me. I'm not speaking of those who, through no fault of their own, have never heard of me. As you yourself know only too well, it's your friends who can hurt you most. Belief in me does not mean accepting a list of facts. It has very little to do with history, which could attempt to prove or dis-prove that I ever walked this earth. It is about being invited on a journey of faith, where many are called but not many choose to follow. The shepherds at Bethlehem were told of my arrival by a group of angels. They responded to that news by saying 'Let us go to Bethlehem, and see this thing for our-selves, which the Lord has made known to us'. If you could imagine the gospels opening with the words 'I invite you all to come and see these things for yourselves. Don't believe anything just because it's in this book. Take the message, put it in practice, and find out for yourself just how real, how transforming, and how life-giving this message is'. It might help you to think of the gospel being in between two sen-tences, 'Come and see' and 'Go and tell'. I certainly need peo-ple who are prepared and willing to go and tell, but I cannot use people who have not come and seen for themselves. Being one of my disciples, one of my followers, is about liv-ing in a certain way, it's about responding on a certain level, it's about having a certain hope, because of what I have said to you and done for you. I came to change your human con-dition utterly and totally. I want to be your source of strength, your inner life, your constant travelling companion on your way back home to the Father. The actual human body I had, the body that was nailed to a Cross on Calvary, that I brought back with me when I returned to my Father. You are now my body, my hands, feet, and voice. I myself continue to be with you, to live in you and, if you let me, to work through you. If you marvel at some of the signs that accompanied my mission on earth, please remember my words that 'greater things shall you do if you are my disciples'.

Because I want to lead you, to accompany you, to travel with you, it is very very important that we have a sense of closeness, and an awareness of being together. I think of you all the time. My Father sent me to find you and to bring you home, so how could I possibly let you out of my sight for one second? If I were to sum up what I want you to know, it would be that you should trust me. I offer you everything you need for now, and for eternity, but nothing happens unless you accept my offer. I respect you totally, and I would never wish to compel you, or to force you into anything. I stand at the door and knock, but the only handle on the door of your heart is on the inside, and I cannot enter until you invite me. I will tell you a secret that will help you understand what I have in mind. You know the stories about Bethlehem, Nazareth, Calvary, Pentecost, etc? If you were out in the Holy Land today, you could visit all those places; you could walk in my footsteps. However, that is not what I really want. What I want, more than anything else, is that your heart should become my Bethlehem, my Nazareth, my Holy Land. That is where I want to live now. There were many closed doors and closed hearts on that first Christmas night. I cannot enter where I am not invited, nor can I make my home, feel at home, or be at home where I am not welcome. That is why I still repeat the words 'I stand at the door and knock'. I'm sure you often heard it said that I came to save the world, to take away the sins of the world. You also have heard the words 'For God so loved the world, that he sent his only-begotten

Son...' These words will never come alive for you unless you apply them directly and personally to yourself. Again and again you need to hear the words 'For God so loved me that he sent his only-begotten Son...' 'Jesus came to save me, and to take away my sins.'

It is very central to my whole plan of salvation that you bring this down to a personal level. 'Who do you say that I am? Will you also go away? Do you love me more than these?' Salvation is balanced in such a way that your freedom of choice is not interfered with in any way. It is my blood and your faith. I have done my part. Quite often, in your prayers, you rightly use the past tense when speaking of my work of salvation. 'Dying, you destroyed our death, rising you restored our life ... By your cross and resurrection you have set us free...' Yes, my part of the work has been done and, on the Cross, I was able to tell my Father that the work he had entrusted to me was now complete. The second part of the programme is the work I entrust to you. Because of my respect for your free-will, I just have to stand outside the door of your heart, and await your response. I offer you salvation, life, healing, and eternal happiness with me, but I can do absolutely nothing about it if you refuse to accept my offer.

I came on this earth to carry out a mission entrusted to me by my Father. That mission was to the lost sheep, to all those who had wandered away from the Garden of Paradise. When Adam and Eve believed the lie of Satan, they came under the control of the father of lies. And they were afraid. I came to invite people back to the Garden, where there is a big hug waiting for them from their Father, the Father of the prodigal children. Again and again, I used the words 'Fear not, do not be afraid. Why are you fearful, oh you of little faith?' I came to lead you back home to the Garden, to where the Father lives, and no one can come to the Father in any other way. I am the Way, the Truth, and the Life. I came that you should have life, and have it to the full. It is not my Father's wish that any of his children should be lost. I take great care of those

entrusted to me by my Father. That is why I compared myself
to a good shepherd. I have been willing to lay down my life
for my sheep. Once again, I remind you of the nature of salvation. I will lead you home, but you must follow. Sheep follow
the shepherd, while the goat-herd has to drive the goats because, by nature, they are not followers. At the end of time I
will separate the sheep from the goats. The gospel is a personal invitation that has R.S.V.P. written all over it. It is an invitation that always calls for a response, even if the response
is refusal or indifference. You are either for me or against me.
All down the years there have been many debates and dis-
cussions about me and what I said, and all the time I am waiting for a decision.

Please continue to think of the gospel as something that is
happening right now, and that you yourself can be every single person there. It is today that I come to you, that I meet
you, that I invite you to follow me. Every single day of your
life is a new invitation. Today I await your Yes of today. I
know you, and understand you through and through. I know
that it is not possible for you to maintain the same level of
commitment day after day. To be human is to ebb and flow, to
fall and rise, to slip and slide. Please do not look for consistency within yourself, or of yourself. The only thing that is
consistent in you is my presence, my Spirit, my love for you.
By your very nature, you are always changing, always evolving, always in the process of becoming. I am leading you towards something, rather than to something. To the day you
die you will always be a human being, someone who fails because you're weak, and not because you're evil. I know you
through and through, and the only barometer in which I am
interested is the readings on your goodwill chart. It is never
about perfection; it is about goodwill, and it is to such people
that I promise peace on earth. When I went looking for others
to follow me, when I called the apostles, I certainly wasn't
searching for perfect human beings, who had it all together,
who knew all the answers, and who were both willing and

capable of saving the world. I looked for people who were human, who were searching, who were lost. I looked for those who had no one to lead them out of the slavery of their human condition, for those who were in bondage to others, or to themselves. I didn't come to condemn, but to save. I came to bring good news, but I always knew that I would be heard only by those who listened, and wanted to hear. My word, my invitation is issued afresh with every new morning. The only yes I am interested in is your yes of now. Following me is never a once-off decision, but a decision that must be renewed with each new day. That invitation will never ever cease, right up to your last breath on this earth. It is never too late. There was a man beside me on another cross on Calvary. He may never have said a prayer in his life but, with his final breath, he asked for help, and I offered him heaven. 'Today you'll be with me in paradise.'

Speak...
Lord Jesus, you are my friend. You told me that you were my friend, and you invited me to be your friend. I have listened to your words of love, and my heart is bursting with excitement at the thought that my God should speak to me, and call me friend. I know I'll never understand this, but I am happy enough that I don't ever have to understand it. All I can do is accept it, and respond to it. Lord, you know me through and through. I don't have to tell you what is happening within my spirit. I don't have to tell you about the guilt, the fears, the shame, and the brokenness that is within my spirit. I don't have to tell you, but neither must I try to deny any of it. All I can do is open out the canvas of my spirit before you, right out to the very edges; to expose to you my inner soul, just as I am, as you see me. I do this with total confidence in your acceptance and love. I know that you will find there the very human conditions you came to set right. I know that you took on our humanity, and I now declare my willingness that you should take on my own personal share

of that humanity, with all its brokenness, and with all its demons. I stand before you now and, in my heart, I consider myself as being each and every person in the gospel. I invite you to enter my heart, and bring the whip of cords with you. I ask you, please, to rid the temple of my heart of everything that is not of you. I ask you, please, to proclaim your victory, to exercise your authority over each and every demon you find lurking within my spirit, whether that be fear, guilt, resentment, or addiction. Please touch my eyes that I might see again; touch my ears that I might listen again; touch my inner being that I might rise up and walk in your ways again. The strongest feeling in my heart at this moment is one of gratitude. I have every reason in the world to be in the depths of despair but, as I stand before you, all of that falls completely away. I have a great sense of being found, of being safe, of being saved. There are times when the burden of my humanity gets to me, and I feel that I'm sinking beneath the lot of it. There are times when my powerlessness discourages me, and my helplessness becomes hopelessness. At a saner moment, like now, I can see much more clearly why and how this happens. I keep forgetting the most important Good News ever announced, and that is that you came on earth to join me in my humanity, to accompany me on the journey, and to bring me safely home. When I hear your words about the Holy Spirit, 'He will remind you of all I have told you', I realise just how much I need to be reminded. I am particularly grateful for the completeness of your message. What I mean by that is that you offer the invitation, and you also offer the grace to respond to that invitation. With the call comes the grace to respond to that call.

I am truly grateful that you know me through and through. So many times, in the gospel, you show that you can read the human mind like a book. Nathanael asked you how you knew him, when he had never met you before. You asked the apostles what they were talking about, as they walked along the road, even though you already knew the answer.

You read the minds of the religious leaders in all their attempts to entrap you, and you left Judas in no doubt that you were very aware of what he was up to. I remember this as I come before you, and I am grateful for the knowledge. There was a time in my life when, like Adam and Eve in the Garden, I wanted to hide. Because of my calling as a Christian, I carry you within my heart and, wherever I go, you are there as well. I often forget this, of course, and becoming more and more aware of this is a very central part of the journey towards conversion, the journey towards truth, freedom, and openness. As far back as I can remember, as a child, I could never disguise my guilt. Even if it didn't show on the outside, I always suspected that the other person must at least suspect. I can only trust your Spirit, and the leadings of the Spirit, but I have begun to notice that, when I am in your presence, I am less and less aware or conscious of guilt. I certainly don't ever want to become callous, indifferent, or to take your love for granted, but all I can do is trust you not to let this happen. I don't want this to happen. I ask you, please, never to let this happen, and then I just leave the rest to you. I have learned over the years that I have no reason to trust myself too much, because I have a mind that can justify or rationalise anything! All I can offer is my goodwill, my sincere prayer and desire, and trust you to protect me from myself.

I am also grateful for how you respect my free-will; how you stand at the door, and await my invitation to enter my heart. I am often more conscious of your trust in me, than of my trust in you. Thank you for that, and for the extraordinary love that is expressed in this way. I know I believe in you, but I'm often puzzled when I consider that you believe in me. We say that hope springs eternal in the human heart, and I believe that that comes directly from the fact that you are living in our hearts. The only honest claim I can make about you being in my heart is my firm conviction that I must surely be one of those you came to save. It has taken me a long time, and I have wandered down many other roads, but at this moment I know and believe that, without you in my heart, I am a lifeless human being, wandering the face of the earth without purpose, direction, or hope. I often reflect on my own journey of faith. I heard the message, and I was told about you from a very early age. It took years, however, to work my way through to some real level of acceptance and belief. Because of my training, I was running to Confession, because I wasn't supposed to be a sinner, and that was something I had to get rid of! As the years went by, and there was no great noticeable difference, it began to dawn on me that this had more to do with my condition than my actions. Once I came to believe I was a sinner, I then came to accept that fact, and I'm only now coming to understand it. This, in turn, has helped me see the great need for you, as my Saviour. Thanks for the patience that is required by all slow learners! I put my hand in yours now, and I want to cling to your grasp and, through thick and thin, I trust you to bring me back safely to the embrace of your Father and of mine.

3. With the Spirit, the comforter

Listen…

How do I speak to you in words that you understand? The Father and Jesus sent me to complete the work of salvation, and I can effect that only through you. You are my voice, my hands, my feet. I'm sure you know by now that only God can do God-things. My role is to supply the power, and your role is to allow that power be in you, flow through you, and work through you. You have a beautiful and perfect model in Mary, the Mother of Jesus. She didn't understand everything, no more than you do. She was asked to follow a way of life that seemed impossible for her. When she asked how this could happen, she was told that I would supply everything that was needed for her to do, and to become all that God had in mind for her. That was all she needed to hear. She was profoundly conscious of her lowliness, of her total inability to lift herself above her human condition. Humility, for her, as for everyone else, was nothing more than accepting the facts of life as they are. It is the freedom to accept truth as it really is. Mary had that gift in an extraordinary way. She wouldn't ever dream of being something or someone she was not. Quite often it is easier for you to understand something better by contrasting it with its opposite, e.g. darkness and light, black and white, full or empty. When someone sees herself as little and insignificant as Mary saw herself, then the thought that the power of the Most High would come upon her is something that would open her whole being to the impossible. She was told that 'There is nothing impossible with God', and she believed that with all her heart. She is just the most perfect, ideal, and very simple model I can hold up before you, as I share with you how I want to work in your life.

From your earliest days, you were told that 'The Blessed Trinity is a mystery, and we can never understand a mystery'. In a way, that's true. On the other hand, as a child of God, you are asked to share in mystery, to experience mystery, and to be part of mystery. There is only one God. That's the basic fact. God, however, can express himself in as many ways and in as many expressions as he chooses. If you look at a cup of water, a snowball, and a lump of ice, you know that what you have is water, even if in different forms. From the beginning, it might help you to think of me as the Breath of God, the breath that was breathed into the clay at the beginning of creation. I was the Presence, the Power of God, who hovered over the waters and brought order out of the early creation. I came upon Mary, so that Jesus could take on human nature, and I came upon the Apostles at Pentecost, which was the birth of the church. I am using this as a simple way to share with you that I have been directly involved in the great significant births in the story of God's people. Although there is but one God, each of us is yet another expression of that simple original fact. The Father is the source of life, the Creator, the one who holds all things in being. The Father is the source of Love and Life, and it might help you to imagine that Jesus and myself are like two giant arms of the Father, reaching out to embrace his children, and bring them safely home to him. Each one of us has a specific role to fulfil, although, because of the unity that comes from love, no one Person of the Trinity would act independently of the other. Jesus said that he never said anything unless the Father told him. He also said that I would come to remind you of all that he had told you, and that I would have nothing further to add to what was already said. Just as I was breathed into the clay (another way of saying this is to speak of the clay being inspired), as I brought order out of the chaos of creation, so I continue to clarify, to inspire, to enthuse, to bring order. Think of me as the Power and Breath of God. Jesus is the one who joined the human race, so that by taking creation, with all its brokenness, back to the Father, everything could be recreated and renewed again. Jesus was sent by the Father to proclaim that the kingdom of God had come on earth. Jesus would be Lord in that kingdom, and his kingdom would never end. Once again, I was directly involved in this process, by inspiring the human clay that Jesus assumed, by leading him as the Father wanted him to go, and by being ready to take over and complete the work, once Jesus had fulfilled his mandate. All of this activity, of creation to re-creation and completion, is the work of the one God, expressed in different ways. For example, let us look at Jesus for a moment. He compared himself to a vine, and his followers to branches. A vine and its branches are of the same genes. For example, I couldn't graft a branch of an oak tree onto an apple tree and expect it to grow apples! If Jesus had not become exactly like you, then you could never be grafted onto him. While still accepting the reality of mystery, I'm sure you'll concede that it may not be so mysterious after all!

I mentioned Mary earlier on. In simple language, Mary didn't actually do anything. She allowed me effect in her all that the Father wanted. Let me explain it to you this way. You are probably fairly familiar with religion. It means being bound by rules that determine behaviour, according to certain norms. It is something external, it is something you do, and it has to do with a certain level of control. Mary was not a religious person, like the Pharisees or the Scribes. With the best of intentions, they were totally committed to what they were doing, and to doing it their way. People like this, however good, easily come to believe that there is no other way, and nothing could or should change, even if God said so! I'm sure you're familiar with the problems Jesus came up against when he tried to deal with such people! Mary, on the other hand, had but one simple belief: I cannot possibly know what is best, I cannot possibly know the mind of God, I can do nothing more than listen, and let God tell me what to do. In simple language, she knew her place, and she let God take care of all the God-things. That is what happened when Gabriel came to her with the message that is called the Annunciation. Once she established that God wanted her to do something, and that he would provide all that was needed to bring that about, she had no hesitation whatever in saying a clear, a simple, and a very definite YES. That is why I hold her up to you as a model, when I speak to you of my love, my plans, and my hopes for you.

As long as civilisation exists, as long as there is human life on this earth, there will always be the need for on-going re-creation, salvation, and redemption. When Jesus did what he came to do, he returned in triumph to the Father. It is important to remember, of course, that the body he had while he walked this earth, also returned with him. And this is where you come in. The task is completed, but it has to be proclaimed, it has to be lived, it has to be witnessed to. I will continue to provide all that is needed, but I need witnesses. I will provide the gifts, but I need someone to carry those gifts, and give them to others. I will provide the power, but I need someone to say the words. I will provide the wisdom, but I need someone to listen with love. If I am to live in your heart, it is because I want to touch the hearts of others through the words you say, the prayers you pray, the life you live, or the very person that you are. If, like Mary, you make yourself available to me, I will supply all you need to know, to do, and to say the things that will complete the building of the kingdom that Jesus brought on earth. My role is to complete that work, and to bring you the fullness of grace. Grace is but another word for gift, and the opposite to sin is grace, and not virtue. In other words, the results are not your responsibility, or the fruits of your own personal endeavour. To put it another way, I want you to be willing to change from religion to spirituality. Spirituality is what I do in you, it is internal, and it is about surrender. This is a fundamental change of heart, a complete conversion of spirit. I'm sure you heard what happened to the Apostles when I came upon them that first Pentecost. Nothing could or would ever be the same again. They were on fire, as it were, and this is the fire that Jesus said he came to bring on this earth.

When Jesus spoke about me, he compared me to a fountain of living water that rises up from within a person. Beneath the driest desert in the world, there is plenty of water. An oasis is a place in the desert where that water has risen to the surface, and it is a source of real life and growth. I want you to be such an oasis in the desert of life. I want you to be someone who is bubbling with inner life and enthusiasm. I want you to be a light in the darkness of this world, to be a resource person who is being lead and, therefore, able to be a leader for others. I want to lead you to live and to walk with my power, to be someone in whom Incarnation is continuous and on-going, to be someone who is evolving into the image of Jesus and, therefore, someone who can sincerely call God Abba, Daddy, Father. I want to inspire everything you do, just as I was breathed into the clay at the beginning. It would be good if you took some time out to reflect on the many things Jesus said about me, the night before he died. He called me the Comforter, the Advocate. A comforter is someone who reassures, who allays fear, who accompanies. You may hear it used in connection with babies, where a comforter can be anything from a dummy, to a blanket, to a teddy. An advocate is someone who speaks or pleads for another. It is important that you grasp this concept, because it has a great deal to do with prayer. There is a vast difference between praying and simply saying prayers. It would be possible to teach a parrot to say a prayer, but it would be impossible to teach a parrot to pray! Does it surprise you to hear that I pray for you all the time, within your heart? If you include me in your words and thoughts, then you are praying. Prayer is a God-thing. How many times have you read in the gospels that one of the prophets, or Zechariah, Mary, Jesus, etc. 'were with the Holy Spirit', and they poured their hearts out in prayer? When I am in your words, then you can be certain that you are praying. Otherwise you might only be saying prayers, and really there is nothing happening. I am always on standby, waiting to be part of everything you do, of every word you say. I cannot enter where I am not invited.

Jesus said that I would teach you, that I would remind you, that I would lead you into truth. This is very central to what I want to do in, through, and for you. The original sin was brought about by the father of lies; therefore, Jesus spoke of me as the Spirit of Truth, as someone who would lead you back from the domain of darkness and deceit, into the kingdom of light and truth. He said that what he had to say would be too much to grasp at any one time, and could only be acquired through an on-going process of revelation. This revelation is a journey of enlightenment, teaching, and leading. That is exactly what I want to effect in you. You know only too well how easy it for you to forget things that are important in your life. That is why Jesus said that I would remind you; I would recall to your mind the things you need to know and to remember. My work in you is continuous, day and night, day in day out. The only condition on your side is to be open to my presence. I love when you turn to me, and include me in everything you do, whether that be praying, writing a letter, or answering a telephone. You are my touch-person in the lives of others. Once you make yourself available to me, then I take full responsibility for everything you need to carry out my work. The gifts that are needed go with the task in hand. In other words, they are not something that is part of your personal possessions. If you are making a decision or advising another, I will supply the gifts of wisdom, discernment, and knowledge for that specific task. In other words, the gifts are made available only when they are needed to carry out my work. If you make yourself available to be my spokesperson, then be assured that your words will be anointed with power. Because the words come from your heart, where I dwell, you can be sure they will enter the hearts of those who hear the words.

St Paul reminds you to 'learn to live and to walk in the Spirit'. Because of your humanity, and the natural tendency to act out of and to think with the mind-set of humanity, it can take some time to bring about the conversion of heart that Paul speaks about. If you think of a child taking its first faltering steps, mumbling its first meaningless sounds, tackling a task that is far beyond its ability, then you get some idea of how you should approach this whole thing. This is a whole new way of being for a human person, because it involves letting go of one's own way of doing things, and learning to live with a power other than one's own. The baby has what it takes to walk, talk, and accomplish many tasks. All that is lacking is the development of those skills, and that is a daily routine of practice. You have what it takes to live and to walk with the power of God, because I am living within the temple of your heart. All you need is the constant daily reminder to use that power, and to walk in my ways. I certainly will always be there for you; I will constantly remind you of my presence, and I will be very very patient in awaiting your response.

Speak...
Holy Spirit, Breath and Power of God, I adore you, I bow down before you, I thank you for making yourself part of who I am, and of including me as part of who you are. Thank you for making your home in my heart, and for making it possible for me to benefit fully from the gifts of salvation, redemption, and Incarnation. For me, you are a go-between God, who makes me part of the life of the Trinity, and there is no honour in heaven or on earth that is greater than that. I am so grateful that I have found you, that I know about you, that I'm coming to know you. Life has afforded me many very definite and clear lessons about the complicities and vagaries of human living, so I don't easily rush in to condemn others

for doing something that has often been part of my own actions. I experience a sense of sadness, however, when I see
others attempting to do something that only you can do, and
that you would willingly do through them. The sadness
comes from the fact that I have been there so often myself,
and I have tried to push huge boulders up mountains for
years, so I can empathise with the frustrations and discour-
agements of others. I'm not responsible for others, so I'll
bring myself back into the centre for the present. It is my honest and sincere desire that I should be totally available to you
at all times, so that you can continue the work of Jesus in me,
and through me. I am very conscious that all I am offering is
my goodwill, and I depend totally on you for everything
after that. Even the goodwill is your gift, so there is nothing
good that has its origins in me. I keep reminding myself that
the spiritual journey is a process, an on-going gestation, an
unending evolution. If I didn't remember this, I would often
be in the depths of despair, when I experience all those things
in me that get in the way of the transformation you are bringing about in me.

In a hymn, we sing to the Father 'You are the Potter, we are
the clay'. I now acknowledge that I am the clay, and that you
are the life; you are the very Breath of God within me. The
very first thing I did when I arrived in this world was to take
a breath into my inner being; and, with one final breath, I will
take leave of this world. Jesus said many simple and beautiful things about you, and the one I am thinking of now is that
he said you would never leave us. Just as you led Jesus into
the desert or into the Temple, I pray that that final breath will
mean you leading me back home to the Father. Only then will
the work of salvation, redemption, and re-creating, begun in
me by Jesus, be brought to its conclusion. If you are to lead
me in the present part of the journey, then surely I want you
to please lead me on that final journey.

In making myself available as an instrument for the building up of the kingdom of God on earth, I know only too well

that I depend totally on you providing the tools, the power, the gifts to do that work. I can provide the readiness, the willingness, and I trust you to provide the gifts. Anything I do or say is nothing more than you working through me. You are part of the Eternal Trinity, the same yesterday, today, and always. Your work is never complete until the kingdom is complete, and the work begun by Jesus is brought to its fulfilment. That, to me, seems to be the will of the Father for his children. I certainly cannot look to myself for any consistency or with any hope of perseverance in doing good. I can depend on you to keep me in a sense of readiness and availability. Jesus said that you would 'remind us', and I can fully appreciate that, because I can so easily forget. My most immediate prayer and longing is to make you the starting-point of all I say, do, or decide. I often think that the kingdom of God is built by contributions that are both small and hidden. It might only be a word, a smile, or a handshake. What makes it material for kingdom-building is that you be present in it. In my everyday living, I am quite familiar with the use of speech. If someone asks me how I am, I am very conscious whether the query is coming out of a genuine concern, or is just a form of greeting. I am very familiar with cynicism, sarcasm, criticism, gossip, or lies. Words convey a spirit, even if only a spirit of indifference. I am very conscious that whatever I say, whatever I do, or whatever I decide, is always influenced by some spirit. That is why I really want to learn to live and to walk with you, so that your presence within me might touch the hearts of those I meet, either through the words I say, the prayers I pray, the life I live, or the very person that I am. I remind myself again and again that you are a fountain of living water within, that you are as near and as central as my own heart. I can so easily get lost up in my head, because I cannot always distinguish intelligence from intellectualism, reflection from analysing, or praying from saying prayers. I believe I am being honest when I say that I'm not looking for perfection for myself, and certainly not of myself. My main concern is that you would continue to recall, to remind, to redirect me towards the truth.

I am conscious that I have always had a genuine respect and reverence for honesty, even when my own words or actions were far from being honest. I think of this as a direct result of the fact that you, the Spirit of Truth, are living within my heart, whether I am conscious of that or not, whether I'm faithful to that or not. Life has taught me the wisdom of the words of Jesus, when he says 'The truth will set you free'. I see you as a direct antidote to the infection of the father of lies, inherited through original sin. It is vitally important for me to think of you, and to consider you as the Spirit of Truth. Because of original sin, I have no reason to trust myself, and to be absolutely sure that I am speaking and living the truth. I live my life in a world of prejudices, bigotry, and intolerance. I was reared on a brand of religion that can easily lead to self-righteousness, giving me a holier-than-thou attitude towards those who do not act as I think they should. The only guarantee I have that I am living and walking in the truth is when I am being led by you. The only certainty that the words I speak are from God is when they are inspired and empowered by you. I believe and accept that one of the effects of original sin is a form of blindness, deafness, and dumbness, that prevents me hearing what I don't want to hear, or seeing what I don't want to see, and that causes me to say that which will bring me some personal advantage. I can never even be sure that I am following your promptings. All I can do is turn to you again and again, offer you my goodwill, and trust you to guide my feet into the path of peace.

I can see how prejudices and bigotry can blind others to reality, and I have no reason to consider myself apart from the rest of humanity. I know that I live in the presence of God at every waking or sleeping moment. I know that I can see evidence of that all around me, if I choose to do so. It bothers me at times when I reflect on how asleep I can be, even during my waking moments. I accept the reality that there can be areas of my life that are totally dormant, and that I can sleep-walk through many a day. I am truly grateful for those moments of disclosure when I am fully alert to the beauty of nature, or the life-giving value of love and friendship. It is at such moments that I am reminded of the other times when I take such things for granted, or am totally unaware of reality. Reality is but another form of truth, and I need your guidance to ensure that I live in reality, and not in some sort of day-dream-land.

The Father sent Jesus to invite us to come back to the Garden. That journey is one of ongoing conversion, one of constant change. For such a journey, there is always need for something to be happening, and I don't always need to be aware of that. I think of this as some form of gestation. When you entered the spirit and soul of Mary something began to happen, and continued to happen. I know and believe that she must have been constantly aware of that. I think of her constant yes to such awareness, which would have kept her spirit in a continual attitude of prayer. I reflect on her prayer of the Magnificat as an outpouring of your presence within her. Her heart was surely a Prayer Room, a Temple, an Upper Room, a Pentecost place. In such places there is always some-thing happening, because of the on-going nature of creation, which involves constant change, constant gestation, constant and continuous life. She was declared to be full of grace, and I think of this as being your presence with all of your gifts. She herself was deeply conscious of the fact that all of this was pure gift, and she could rightly sing that 'He that is mighty has done great things for me, and holy is his name'. I cannot at all hope to have her profound sense of lowliness, which meant that she was empty of all selfishness, self-seeking, and self-advancement. All I can do is ask you, please, to continue your work in me. I often think of myself as a deep deep well, where you are a gurgling spring of living and life-giving water down at the base of that well. My problem is that life has filled the well with its own wreckage and garbage. I trust

you to work in me so that, one by one, each and every one of
those defects and shortcomings may be brought to the surface, and disposed of. I don't honestly expect that this will
happen in the time remaining to me on this earth. All I cling
to is my hope in the process; in other words, that some of that
is happening right at this very moment. I have no options, I
have no alternatives. Unless you work in me, I can never be
redeemed from the control of the power of darkness, deceit,
and death. With all my heart I say yes, yes, yes, again and
again, and leave the rest to you. Thank you for being with
me, for being in me, for accompanying me on the journey.

4. Mary, my Mother

Listen…

My child, you are very precious to me. While I walked the earth, I wasn't at all fully aware of what God's plan was for me, for you, for the world. The only thing of which I was absolutely certain was that there was nothing I myself could do to change the world, or the human condition. For his own purposes, God chose me to be a channel of his grace, of his peace, of his person. I have never thought it necessary that I should question that, doubt that, or even try to understand that. At the beginning, of course, I asked some questions … 'How can this happen? … Why did you do this to us?', but it was revealed to me that, while I might ask the questions, I did not need to know the answers. My role was to be, to be still, to open my hands and my heart, and let God be God. I sometimes thought that God had chosen me simply because he could have chosen anyone. I have no doubt that God could have chosen anyone, and I now simply accept the fact that he chose me. I was given the great grace of being able to live with mystery. Life is a mystery to be lived, and I was always conscious of the on-going revelation of that mystery. In simple language, I didn't know, and never needed to know, what God would do next or what would be asked of me. I never saw that as necessary. I was given the grace to be available, and leave all the decisions to God. I felt that my role was to be an instrument, and I was freed from the need to understand all that that meant. I had no reason whatever to doubt that God knew what he was doing, and that is all that mattered to me. I rejoiced in the privilege, while being free from concern

about the outcome. The only choice I had, and the only decision I made, was to say yes and then trust that the promises
of the Lord would be fulfilled in me. If the Holy Spirit was to
come upon me, and the power of the Most High was to over-
shadow me, then I saw no reason for any worry or concern on
my part.

My life with Jesus was one continuous revelation. I lived
in my heart, and I pondered the words and the events there.
As a human being, I do not believe that I could live a mystery
up in my head. All of what was happening was too vast for
me to comprehend, so I could just watch and pray. My faith
wasn't always some sort of blind faith, because it would not
be possible to live in the continuous presence of God and not
see glimpses of divinity. It was a response to some deep
awareness of the divine presence that prompted me at Cana
to ask for a miracle. It was many years before when I was told
that 'nothing is impossible to God'. I had always believed
that, but it was then that I acted on it, and I was not at all surprised at the miracle. In my daily living, I considered my life
as one constant miracle. If God could do what he had done
with me, I had no reason to doubt that he could do anything
with anybody, or anything else. Because my life involved
constant insight and revelation, I had come to expect the
signs of God's presence, and the results of that presence. I
tried not to get in the way, to do God's work for him, or to set
limits to what he could do through and with me. So many
times, in your own life, for example, the only limitations of
what God can do in you, through you, and for you, are the
limitations that are set by you.

My earlier life had been spent in the environs of the
Temple, so I was used to the presence of the Holy of Holies. I
was familiar with sacrifices, as blood-offerings for the forgiveness of sin. I was familiar with the concept of the lamb of
sacrifice and, the more I listened to Jesus, the more aware I
was that he, in his own person, was the Lamb who had come
to clear the debt and the divisions that alienated people from

God. I thought of him as having one hand in the hand of the Father, and the other hand held out to all of the children of God. As a mother, my heart was pierced when I saw both hands nailed to a cross, and my dearly beloved son suspended between heaven and earth. This is where my journey of faith was also a journey of great pain and suffering. Because of the nature of events, I knew Jesus through and through. I knew his extraordinary love, his unbounded zeal, his immense compassion. I knew his deep commitment to the mission on which he had come, and his single-minded determination to bring that mission to its completion. Unlike Peter, I never tried to persuade him, or to deter him from doing what he had come to do. Somewhere within myself I had a clear pre-monition of where all this would lead. With each day I pon-dered on the promises, and at each stage of the journey I just whispered my yes. I would be there for him, wherever that would lead, and I was there with him on Calvary. On that hill I saw much more than my son dying. I saw the extraordinary strength, depth, and scope of his love. I saw the ugliness of sin, and the extremes my son went to in order to nail sin to the cross. He became sin, as it were, and he hung on that cross on behalf of and in the place of every sinner, and of every sin that was ever committed. Deep within my spirit, which was pierced with anguish, I pondered on what I witnessed, as the earth went dark, the graves were opened, the dead arose and appeared to many. It was no surprise to me to learn that the veil of the Temple was rent in two. Surely such a supreme sacrifice must have made it possible for all of God's children to enter the Holy of Holies, to come directly into the presence of God, without fear of condemnation. On Calvary I wit-nessed the greatest event that ever happened on this earth since the Creation and the Fall. I never felt within myself any need to understand what was happening. I had long since come to know my place before God, and I was present, I said my yes, and I pondered in my heart all that had happened up till now. On Calvary, I just had to cling to faith in the darkness

of that moment, and trust, and trust again that all would be
well, whatever happened. I was aware of the evil in the air. I
was aware that the evil one had marshalled all his forces to
destroy the one person on this earth who could overcome the
evil, and undo the harm of the lie that was told in the Garden.
I had witnessed the attacks of Satan in many other ways, and
I was fully aware that my son had complete authority over
him. On this occasion, however, evil was being seen to triumph, and that was something I was absolutely certain could
not happen. I didn't know how the situation was going to be
reversed but, as I said already, I never saw it as my role to
know or to understand. For me, faith always meant moving
forward in trust, and letting time confirm that what I did was
right. Faith was always something more tangible and more
real than just belief. Faith came from what I experienced or
witnessed myself, rather than from some personal opinion. If
Jesus said it, I accepted and believed it, and that was always
enough for me. That is why, my child, that it is so centrally
important, no matter how bad things may seem, no matter
how much one may fail, or no matter how victorious evil is
seen to be, the only real sin for a Christian is to lose hope, and
not believe that all will be well, that evil will eventually be
destroyed, that goodness will have the final and eternal triumph.

I was not at all surprised, then, when I met Jesus on Easter
Sunday morning. It was not for me to know how this could
happen. All I had was his word that he would rise again, and
my own heartfelt belief that evil, even if seen to be triumphant for a while, can never overcome goodness. It was a
joyful reunion. On Calvary, I understood that he wished to
involve me even more in the proclaiming and building of his
kingdom. The apostle John, whom Jesus entrusted to my care
with his last breath, represented to me all of God's children.
On that Easter morning I could clearly see what my role
would be. Jesus had spoken many times about returning to
the Father, and sending the Holy Spirit to complete his work,

and, somehow, I felt that this is where I would come in. That Spirit had been with me all my life and, in a more special way, at the most significant moments. I was well aware just how weak and how human the apostles were. Despite everything Jesus had said, despite every miracle they saw him work, despite all the time they had spent with him, when the crunch came, they sold him, denied him, or deserted him. I knew that even his risen presence among them would not be enough to change their basic insecurities, or allay their inner fears. Because of my own personal experience of the power, presence, and effect of God's Spirit in my own life, I knew they needed a total change of heart, a complete re-creating process, and that is what happened at Pentecost.

The Upper Room was a very joyful experience for me. I had held Jesus in my arms as a baby, and as a corpse. I now knew that, once the Spirit came, and the Body of Christ was made present among us again, that I would be directly involved in the process. At heart, the apostles were good decent human beings. At the Last Supper Jesus had called them his friends, and they were certainly my friends. My best help for them at this juncture was to assure them again and again that, yes, the Spirit would come. I'm not sure they all believed that as the days passed! All I could give them was my own unshakeable trust that Jesus would keep his promise, and that helped them endure the waiting. We prayed together, and I was able to help them to join their hearts and their minds in the prayer, so that we did actually pray with one mind and one heart. We got to a stage where I suppose you could say that the Spirit came because he was expected to come! As the days past by, the apostles' hopes were rekindled, and their hurts were healed. They were thrilled to meet Jesus again at Easter, but then he left them again, and many of their fears resurfaced. They had all suffered their own hurts along the way, even if most were of their own making. Pentecost was like a whole new creation. It was as if the snows had melted, the darkness was gone, and all of nature was in full bloom again. I sang my Magnificat many times over as I saw the transformation that came about in them. They were changed utterly, and it was a foretaste of heaven to see the light in their eyes and the glow on their faces. The final stage of the mission of salvation could now begin. The Spirit had come and, just as I was asked to provide the body at the beginning, they now would provide the body, the hands, the feet, and the voice, to proclaim that Good News. They went forth to witness to the Good News of Jesus, to proclaim his salvation, and to exercise the power that had been entrusted to them. My own journey was now complete, and I longed with each breath to rejoin Jesus in the New Jerusalem.

How do I explain my role in your life? Where do I begin? As the Spirit was present at all the significant births in the history of the world, from Creation to Incarnation to Pentecost, so must he now effect a whole new birth in you. Jesus entrusted you to me as a very precious child, whom I now love just as much as I have ever loved him. Like any mother, I care for all my children, and I want what is best for all. I want nothing less for you than the blessings I myself received when the Spirit of God came upon me, and the power of the Most High overshadowed me. I want to take up residence in your heart, so that you too can have your own Bethlehem, your own Pentecost. I want to embrace you, to hold you, and to bring you into full membership of the family of God. I want to share my faith with you, and I want to pray with you, for you, and in you. Like any mother, I want to teach you the basics of walking, of talking, and of living by the power of the Spirit. As the caretaker of your heart, I want to turn to Jesus, just as I did at Cana, and obtain the miracle you need at any one time. I want to be part of your journey, and my greatest longing is to have all my children back safely home again. I want to protect you from the evil one who declared war on all of my children. I have been given the power to crush his head, and he has no power over those upon whom I cast my mantle. Incarnation, salvation, and redemption is on-going, and it must happen within the heart of each person on this earth. Like that first Christmas night, there are still many hearts and homes closed and unwelcoming. My heart is one with the heart of Jesus, and I rejoice with him when any one of his children turns or returns to him. I share in all the heavenly rejoicing when the door of another heart is open, so that I can witness yet again all the signs and wonders that I lived with as I walked this earth. Like Jesus, I, too, stand at the door and knock.

Speak...
Mary, my dear dear Mother, thank you, thank you. It's wonderful to think and to know that you're there. Within all of us is the Inner Child, always in need of a mother. Despite all the bravado and the 'grown-up' behaviour, I know that you see the child within. What amazes me is the possibility that you see that child, which is me, exactly as you saw your son Jesus. It is not easy for my mind to comprehend the fact that you are my mother, every bit as much as you are his. I grasp at the possibility that Jesus had you in mind when he asked us to become like little children. I know, of course, that he was also referring to the Father, but he certainly wasn't inviting us into a one-parent family. Putting you into the formula changes things completely. You were the human instrument used by God to make incarnation possible. You were the one chosen to provide the body, and the humanity, which God would take on, in which he would live, and through which he would effect our redemption. In other words, you were the one opening in the whole jungle of humanity where God was free to enter, and in whom he could make his home. Because of freewill, the rest of humanity could close the door, and even God could not or would not enter. If there was to be a whole new humanity created, then you were chosen to have a part in that creation, in that re-creation, in that redemption. You are not God, you are not Redeemer, you are not divine; nor did you ever claim to be anything other than a simple ser-

vant, who was available to do whatever God asked of you. You were very central, essential, and necessary, though, if God were to come among us, to assume our human nature, and undo all the evils that had entered his original creation. I have no doubt that God could have chosen any other way of doing things, or any other person as his instrument, and that, in his infinite wisdom, he deliberately selected you. Jesus would be the new Adam, and you would be the new Eve and, this time, it would go strictly according to the will of God. Things would be done God's way, we would know our proper place before God, and we could live and share in the very life of God. The final and definitive march back into the Promised Land had begun, for those who chose to follow. The whole three Persons of the Trinity would be involved and, in a very unique way, you yourself would be personally involved by them in every step of the journey. You represented the good wheat the farmer sowed. You were still good wheat, while being surrounded by the weeds of sin, sickness, and death on every side. When I was growing up, I was familiar with seeing a scare-crow out in the middle of a field of wheat. No, I don't think of you as a scare-crow! Rather I think of you as Ruth in the wheat fields as recorded in the Old Testament. In simple language, you stick out among the weeds; the contrast is stark and clear. You escaped the contamination, the virus, the evil, and you truly were our human nature's solitary boast.

The Father chose you; you accepted with open heart the outpouring of the Spirit, and the Word, Jesus, assumed human nature through you. Because he is God, Jesus could assume the whole of humanity within himself, and the results of whatever he would do with that would be made available to anyone who chose to accept it. In this re-creation, you became Mother of the new Creation. Once I accept Jesus as my personal Saviour, as the one who has come to bring me safely back to the Father, then, by that very fact, I enter into all of what we call the New Covenant, the new and eternal agreement offered to us who are wandering through the desert of life. When I say YES to that, I accept God as Father, Jesus as Moses, the Spirit as the Power to walk in the path of Jesus, and you as the mother who holds my hand along the way. I love nature programmes on the telly. It never ceases to amaze me to watch the mother-instinct at work, even among the most primitive of creatures. I love watching how the young are protected, fed, and reared. This scene becomes more remarkable when it involves a baby elephant, a baby giraffe, or a baby ostrich. The mother is so huge compared to the new-born, and yet the little one is at the very centre of her attention. This does not reflect how I think of me travelling along with you! There is a vast difference here, and this is because of you. I am, indeed, the weak, wobbly, wandering one; but you, because of your extraordinary humility, are able to be with me as I am, and I don't at all feel over-powered in your presence. In my present existence, I have a sense of now-but-not-yet, of being on the way, in process, in a state of gestation, awaiting something beyond my wildest dreams. At times, I think of you carrying me in your womb; at other times, you are living as caretaker of my heart and, at other times, you are walking beside me, holding my hand. In some mysterious way, I'm sure, it often involves all three at any one time. Whatever it is, there is one thing I ask: Please keep me very very close to you. Don't let me out of your sight, and continue to bring me closer and closer to Jesus, so that I can become more and more like him.

There are so many graces I need that I wouldn't know where to start! The one that comes to mind at the moment, as being of primary importance, would be to know my place before God. You magnified the Lord, and your God was so omnipotent and magnificent that you, yourself, felt like a tiny grain of sand in his presence. Because you clearly knew your place before God, you were fully open to miracle. You had no problem with the words 'Nothing is impossible with God'. When the angel brought you God's request, and you were as-

sured that all of this would happen because the Holy Spirit
would come upon you, and the power of the Most High
would overshadow you, you had no problem whatever with
saying YES. There were two things of which you were certain: You could do nothing, and God could do anything. I believe this as proof that you were totally preserved from the
lies of Satan, from the effects of original sin. For you, those
two certainties were so obvious but, because of original sin,
we have some sort of blindness of spirit that prevents us seeing things as they really are. There are times when I get a little
glimpse or insight into what you always saw so clearly.
Please, please, pray for me, that my realisation of this truth
might continue to grow. If I knew my place before God, I
could be as I really am, without need or nudge to pretend, to
impress, or to be anything other than who and what I am, before God and before people. I would discontinue all attempts
at playing God, or of doing all those many many things that
only God can do. I would stand back and let him that is
mighty do great things for me. Like John the Baptist, as I
begin to decrease, God can continue to increase, and miracles
become events that I witness and depend on, rather than
something I vaguely hope for. When I think of Cana of
Galilee, I can understand how that first miracle came about.
You saw the problem. You could do nothing about it. But you
knew that Jesus had access to the power of God and, therefore, there was no reason why there should not be a miracle.
Your faith was simple, trusting, and totally uncomplicated,
and it had nothing of the arrogant, the demanding, or the ma-
nipulative about it. What a wonderful gift! I ask you, please,
to go to Jesus on my behalf. My faith is like water, and I don't
have any wine ...

I think of you as a person of the heart. You were never a
heady person, trying to figure out, to analyse, or to understand. You heard the word, and you pondered that word in
your heart. Your heart was an Upper Room, a Prayer Room, a
Pentecost Place and, when you heard a word from God, you

took that word to your heart, pondering on what it might mean. This was at the very centre of your prayer and your praying. The word of God was continually becoming flesh in and through you. That is why I need you as caretaker of my heart. I invite you, please, to take up residence there, to make my heart your home, to obtain and supervise the on-going miracle of incarnation within me, so that the Word of God, Jesus, might be formed within me. I think of you in my heart as you were when the Spirit came upon you in Nazareth, or at Pentecost. I make my heart available for that on-going, endless, creative action of God's Spirit, until the work of redemption is completed within me. Of myself, I have everything that can block, mess up, oppose, and prevent everything that Jesus came to do. I think of his grace building on my human nature, rather than replacing it. Therefore, the original problem, the original sin, the strong impulse to be God and to play God, is still there. Like any child, I need someone to trust, someone I can depend on, someone who is there for me. That is how I see you, and how I think of you. This does not exclude Jesus, his Father, or the Spirit, of course. I think of you in a different way. You were 100% human, and you did perfectly everything that I am struggling to do. Whereas Jesus, as God, came down among us, you came from among us. To me it may be very far-fetched but I'm sure, to you, it is acceptable: If God had a YES from me, like he had from you, he could do the very same things through me. In fact, I think of that as being my very calling, despite all the obstacles I find or place in the way. Because you are my mother, and you have a mother's heart, I can tell you just how much I would love to be open to God, and I know you will understand. In human language, and with human reasoning, my ideas are crazy, I know, but I also know that nothing is impossible with God. I trust you, please, to help me along the way, to pray for me, with me, and in me, so that, at least, I may move in the right direction. I have no reason to trust myself. When I began school, or when I first went to a dentist, my mother came with me, and that made all the difference. I constantly need that awareness of accompaniment. It scares me to think of myself wandering on my own, depending on my own instincts to guide me in the right direction.

As caretaker of my heart, I look to you to supervise and provide the conditions for Pentecost to take place there. I can identify with the Apostles as you all gathered in that Upper Room. They were a broken bunch. Despite all they had heard and seen, when the crunch came, they ran, they denied, they failed miserably. I myself could honestly feel very much at home among them! They needed your strength, they needed your faith. Jesus promised to send the Spirit, and so the Spirit would certainly come. I could imagine you saying that to them again and again. Like Peter or Thomas, I too can easily become restless when I'm waiting for something to happen! You, however, could assure and reassure them that, even in the waiting, there is always something happening. The journey itself is part of the arriving; the foundations must be laid before the house can be built. From your perspective of God, I feel that waiting was a real expression of your faith. For the poor among us, waiting is part of everyday living ... waiting in line for food, for money, for hand-outs, for help. The wealthy never have to queue for anything. You were poor, totally poor in spirit, and waiting for God was an expression of your faith. The important thing, though, and the one that makes all the difference, is that you lived with expectation, with constant hope. Even at the lowest point, as on Calvary, you lived with the belief that all would be well, whenever and however God decided. You were led by the Spirit, and you never ran ahead of God into all the worries and questions about to-morrow. I think of you as quietly repeating your YES each at every moment, with each and every development.

Mary, Mother, there are times when I feel embarrassed as I stand before you. As I was growing up it was important to

me that my mother be pleased with me, and even proud of
me. When she did die, I remember thinking 'Now she really
knows what I'm really like!' I know, of course, that her love
didn't change, and her view of everything would have
changed fundamentally as she shared fully in the compassion and understanding that is part of how God sees us.
When I stand before you, however, I know, right now, that
you know me through and through and, because of the mother-
love in your heart, you want everything that's best for me. I
don't at all feel condemned in your presence, but I often get a
certain sense of letting you down, and failing to avail of, and
to make use of the many many graces offered to me by Jesus.
I imagine, if I were sitting speaking with you, that you would
speak with such love and conviction about how much the
Lord needs our availability and co-operation, and what wonders the Spirit can do in the hearts and lives of those who are
open to his presence and his power. All I can do is continue to
offer myself, continue to make myself available, continue to
reach out for your hand, by way of assurance, and continue
to hope that all will be well, and all manner of things will be
well.

5. The return of the Prodigal

Speak…

'I will arise now, and return to my Father's house.' I accept the Good News of the gospel. I know only too well that I am one of the sinners whom Jesus came to find, to redeem, and to lead safely back home to the Garden. Yes, indeed, I have wandered away down many a side-path, I have given free rein to self-will run riot, and I have put myself and my own selfish agenda at the top on many occasions. I am thankful, Lord, for the gifts you have given me, even if I have not always used them for the building of the kingdom. I have used my tongue to hurt and to deceive; I have used my mind and my heart to harbour resentments, angers, jealousies, and self-centred ideas.

Father, I know that I have allowed the evil one to lead me further away from the Garden. I fell for the lie and the allurement of sin, I chose not to heed the inner voice of conscience, and I protected myself, at times, with a cloak of indifference. I think of you looking off into the distance, watching for signs of my return. The love with which you created me is still fully aglow, and all your hopes and expectations for me are still fully alive. It frightens me to think that, because of free-will, I can continue to wander away, and no matter how much you long for my return, I can walk away from you for all eternity. I think of the gospel as you sending Jesus, the messenger, inviting us to return to the banquet, to the celebration of life, to the celebration of love. 'Father I am not worthy to be called your child.' I know, of course, even if I never left the embrace of your love, that I am still not worthy of such an extraordinary gift. I sometimes experience a certain fear and anxiety that I might take you for granted, as if I had some claim on you, or you owed me something. I thank you, Father, that I know you, that I can speak to you, that I have listened to Jesus' words about you. In that sense, I do feel special, privileged and chosen, and I don't understand why. There are many who don't know you, and there are others who don't want to know you. I don't understand why you should have sent Jesus to me personally, and I don't want or need to understand. When I think of your love, and the practical down-to-earth love expressed by Jesus, and then I examine my own behaviour, I have all the reason in the world to be grateful.

Father, you are the creator, the sower of the good seed. You can see the weeds in me that are not part of your creation. You sent Jesus to remove those weeds, so that what remains of me could be gathered into your barns. Like St Paul, I often experience something deep within that rebels against my better self, and overcomes my good intentions and resolutions. That is one of the weeds, called sin, that are not of your creation. I open my heart to the fullness of your Spirit, that sin might be removed from my heart, and that I may be washed in the Blood of the Lamb, your Son Jesus. Father, I do want to belong in your family, and I want to be free from everything that would alienate me from your family. There are drives, impulses, compulsions, addictions, and attachments within me that frighten me at times. I can look at the most public criminal and know – 'There but for the grace of God go I.' Father, I can identify with the Prodigal Son; but what frightens me even more, I can find myself in the role of his self-righteous brother. In my heart I know that I cannot afford to throw a stone at anyone, but that doesn't seem to stop me doing so, when the opportunity arises.

Father, I know, of course, that I have not yet reached your house, that I am still very much on the way. As you look off into the distance, I believe you can see me coming. Father, please guard my every step along the way, because I am so wont to wander, to dally, to be distracted, and to risk getting lost. As a child of a loving Father, I owe nothing to this world, or its allurements. I accept you as the one true God, and I accept Jesus, whom you have sent. What I ask for, please, is that, through the working of your Spirit, I might be given a new heart. I ask you, please, to remove this heart of stone, and to breathe your Spirit into me. I have a deep-felt need for a total inner transformation that will direct my steps towards you, and in the path opened up for me by Jesus. Father, when the Prodigal returned, you insisted that he be fitted out with sandals, which was a declaration that he was free to leave again if he so chose. You will never take away our freedom to make decisions or to have choices. It is one of life's greatest mysteries that you should entrust to us so much responsibility for our own eternal welfare. The more I think of it, though, the more I come to understand your love, your way of loving, and your way of doing things. You know me through and through. You know my every thought, longing, and desire. You offer me everything that will make my life here on earth of such a quality that it will take on eternal possibilities. You offer unconditional love, and unconditional forgiveness. You offer me full membership in your family, where I can call you Father, and call Jesus Brother. You offer me the very same Spirit that was breathed into the clay at the beginning of creation, so that I can be re-created and made new again. Your offers are endless, enduring and eternal; and yet, you still insist that all final decisions and choices be mine. It is really difficult for a human mind to understand such unlimited, boundless love. In our world, we are used to trading favours, to meeting requirements, to paying and repaying debts. We are familiar with pressures, with manipulation, with blackmail of various kinds. There is a price-tag on everything, and there is a line beyond which human love cannot pass. It is difficult for us not to tie you in with our ways of doing things. I always need reminding that you are God, for whom nothing is impossible, and that your ways are not our ways.

Father, I come before you now, exactly as I am. Like the Prodigal, I have gone my own way, and done my own thing. I have wasted many of your gifts, including the gift of time. I have lived without a thought of you, and I have assumed your rightful place in my life, on those many occasions when I have tried to play God. The very fact that I'm turning to you now is evidence that my ways have never satisfied my heart, or given me peace. I want to return to you, where I belong. I have sinned against heaven, and before you, and I am not worthy to be called your child. I ask your forgiveness, and I ask that, through the Blood of Jesus, and the work of your Spirit, my heart might be cleansed, my inner being might be renewed, and my proper belonging in your family be fully restored.

Listen…

Welcome, welcome home into the heart of my family, my dear dear child. I have watched your every step, and your heart has always been before me. I sent Jesus to bring you back. If your sins are like scarlet, I will make them white as snow. I sent Jesus to save, to invite, and not to condemn. I give you my Spirit of Truth to lead you away from the power of the evil one, the father of lies. I embrace you with great joy. Like the Prodigal, you are always free to leave again. I want you to make your home with me, to be at home with me, and to feel at home with me. You are back where you belong. Jesus has paid the price, to redeem you from slavery, and I want you to experience the freedom of the children of God.

The greatest thanks you can give me for sending Jesus is to accept all that he died to earn for you. As God, Father, Son, and Spirit, we rejoice in your goodwill. We never ever want to take away your free-will, and we understand your human condition in a way that would be entirely impossible for the human mind to comprehend. We are so much less interested in what you do, than in why you did it; in who you are, than in how you act. It is what is going on in your heart that gets our full attention. We, the Trinity, have made our home in you, and we want you to know that your heart is a holy place, a sanctuary, a place of divine indwelling. It is from within your heart that we wish you to change. This is not possible for you. You can do everything within your power to improve your outward behaviour, to control your compulsions, to harness your emotions … and all to no avail. Your healing, your redeeming, your power, and your life must come from our presence within your heart. Thinking of Mary as the caretaker of your heart can help you accept the possibility of miracles there. When you return to me, you are returning to your heart. Look at yourself in the mirror sometime. Study what you see there. If you can really forgive the person looking out at you from that mirror, then you are getting in touch with the forgiveness already available within.

Spend some time thinking of the function of the human heart; how totally dependent the rest of the body is on it; and how its every beat is ensuring that your life continues. Move then to think of the heart, not as something physical, but as that part of you where you are most yourself, that inner part of you that is at the very core of your being. That is where the evil one had penetrated, that is where we choose to make our home; that is where the battle is fought. It is here that your basic choices must be made. You can choose good or evil, life or death. Choose life, and you will receive life in abundance. Go to this place of your being with your decisions, your choices, and your prayers. For you to go to this place is for the Prodigal to come home. The journey to the heart is the journey home.

The conflict between good and evil will always continue within you, until your journey is complete, and you are free, free, free at last. It would not be good for you if the conflict were removed, because that is part of human life, and it is in and through the conflict that growth takes place. Experiencing your own weakness is the school where compassion is learned. Your inner being is but part of the worldwide struggle between good and evil. There is very little happening out there that is not reflected, in some way, within your own being. Because your heart is the home of the Trinity, however, you live with this sure and certain hope: evil can never overcome the good, even where it is seen to be successful for a while. The only real sin for you is not to have hope, not to live with the certain belief that, in the end, when the kingdom of Satan and the kingdom of the world come to an end, there will remain forever and ever the kingdom of God. Because of what Jesus has done, your name is registered as a citizen of that kingdom and, unless you deliberately and irrevocably decide to tear up the passport, you will live in that kingdom forever.

6. Heal me, Lord

Speak...

Lord Jesus, one of the things that always amazes me is how so many of the sick, in the gospel stories, actually believed that you could and would heal them. I know they may have heard of others being healed, and they may have actually seen others being healed, but the certainty of their conviction always amazes me. Since that time, two thousand years later, we have been anointed with your Spirit, we are part of your Body, we are members of a believing community, and we have had two thousand years to reflect on your words. Surely we, of all people, should live with the faith of conviction, with the expectation and the reality of miracles!

I realise that, in the gospel, you yourself had not yet carried your cross, you had not died, you had not yet returned in triumphant glory to your Father. As you said 'When the bridegroom is present, you are not asked to fast; but when the bridegroom is taken away from you, then you shall fast'. I take this to mean that, when you have carried your cross, when your work is completed, when we have received the Spirit, when we answer the call to follow you, then we too, must take up our own cross and walk in your way. I accept that this is a call to suffering; not involving any great heavy cross, but the splinters of daily Christian living. I know, and I accept, that some of what we have to suffer is for our good, and that we are purified, and brought closer to you, through it. I look upon this as a vocation, as a calling, and I have known of people whose whole life was a call to suffering. That, however, would seem to be a special calling to special people, and with the call comes the grace to live in that way.

All of us, at some time or another, are called to put our shoulder to the cross, and the proof that such is the case is the evidence of the good that results from such suffering.

Why I come before you now is to ask your healing for sickness, for something that seems to produce no good results; something that burdens my life and, indirectly, is affecting those who love me and those whom I love. I come to you, Lord, because, with all the best medical attention in the world, you are the only one who can make me well again. I believe, Lord, help my unbelief. Lord, increase my faith. Lord, I know that you can heal me. Of that I am certain. I also know that, beyond your great love, I have no claim on your healing. I stand before you, open out my heart, and let you see each and everything within me, body, mind, heart, and soul. I am sure you see many areas there in need of healing. I'm sure you see healing needed where I don't suspect any lack of health, either physical, mental, or spiritual. Lord, please, what you see in me that is not of you and from you, and that is not for my good, I ask you to touch that now, to heal it, remove it, and fill that space with new health and life. Say but the word, Lord, and I shall be healed.

Lord Jesus, I bow my head before you, and I reach out both hands towards you. Place your healing hand upon me, and proclaim your power and victory over anything that would take from my well-being. I fully accept that we must all, one day, die. I also accept and appreciate the gift of life, and would really love to live a full, fruitful and abundant life. I ask for your healing, because to whom else can I go? You, and you alone, have the power over life, health, and death. I open the door of my heart and, as with Peter's mother-in-law, Jairus, Zacchaeus, and many others, I invite you to enter with your healing and restoring touch. Lay your hands gently upon me, O Lord; let them bring your forgiveness and healing. I claim the power of your victory, your Blood, and your name, and I cry out to you, Lord. Jesus, son of David, have mercy on me! Lord, if you will, you can make me whole.

Lord, I am not worthy; say but the word, and I shall be healed.

I trust your Spirit within me to give life to my words, to turn my words into prayer. I know that a cry from my heart will always reach your heart. I often feel so weak, so inadequate, and this creates its own confusion. I hesitate to ask, because I don't want to ask for anything that is not for my good, or for something that is not your will for me. The only way I can manage that, Lord, is to come right out and ask, and leave the answer to you. I believe that you always answer prayers, and that sometimes the answer is NO. That is why I dare to keep on asking, because there is nothing else I can do. I cannot trust myself to judge what is best for me, or what your will for me is. I have to continue to trust you, to ask you, to turn to you, because you are the source of all that is healthy in me, and I know that you take me seriously. I believe that you have my best welfare at heart, that you understand exactly how I feel, how I fear, and how I falter. I don't find it easy to be brave, and not to be in control. I may pretend with others that all is well, but you know me through and through, and you know exactly how I feel inside. You know my prayer even before I say it. You know my doubts, my anxieties, and my worries, even when I try to convince myself that I trust you. I sometimes get confused over faith, as if it were a question of me having faith in my own faith. Some sort of white-knuckle, gritted teeth, clenched fist type of prayer, as if I could force you to change your mind, and do things my way! I'm sorry for the times when I do that, and I know you understand. The healing has nothing to do with me beyond the two basic facts: I am sick, and I am asking you to heal me. I totally rely on your Spirit to inspire and infuse my words, and to turn them into prayer. I also ask for the grace of being able to leave this prayer with you, and get on with life. I think of the ten lepers who left and were healed as they went along. I think of the centurion who took your word for it, and returned to find his servant healed.

Lord, please come with me now, and travel with me on the road of faith. Keep me close to you, Lord, and stay close to me. Lift me when I falter, and like Peter walking on the water, be there, please, to reach out a hand to hold me up when I feel that I'm going under. If you travel with me, Lord, it must surely lead to health and to life.

Listen...

My dear dear child, I hear your cry, and I know your fears and your tears. Thank you for coming to me with your cares and worries. Come to me when you are struggling, or heavily burdened, and I will give you rest, and you will find peace for your soul. I know how difficult it can be to really trust another. I trusted the Apostles and, when the crunch came, they deserted me. With me, however, it is so much different. All I ask for is faith. Nothing more, nothing less. 'The sin of this world is unbelief in me. When the Son of Man comes, will he find any faith on this earth?' Faith is much simpler than you think. It is a direct response to love. In other words, it is the trust you place in someone who loves you. If you believe that I love you, then you should have little trouble in trusting me. In this is love, not that you love me, but that I have first loved you. That was the whole purpose of my coming on earth. The only response I ask is that you trust me. I want you to ask me, and I have declared for all the world to hear: 'Ask and you will receive, seek and you will find, knock, and the door will be opened to you.' In the gospel stories, it is not that I went around healing anybody. Rather was it a case that I went around, with the power to heal, and I left it totally to the blind, the lame, the deaf, the dumb, or the leper to stop me and ask for healing. All I looked for from them was that they believed that I could cure them. Having that faith within themselves was the foundation of their healing. If that were missing, my power could not work in them, because that would be to intrude on them, to trespass on their privacy and freedom to choose not to be healed. That is why I asked the man at the well 'Do you want to be healed?' Up to that point he hadn't asked me, and I needed to hear him express his prayer.

Prayer is when you spend time with me, when you give me time and space in your life. It is a time of friendship, when a relationship is built. Communication is two-way or no-way. It is important that you speak, but it is also important that you listen. I want to know your every concern, your every worry, your every fear. I like when you trust me enough to turn to me. Being in my presence, being present to me, is in itself healing. I want you to be healthy. I want you to be well. I don't want anything bad to happen to you. I only want what is best for you. You are my friend, and you did not choose me, but I have chosen you, and I have appointed you to bear fruit, fruit that will remain. No one wants fruit that is unhealthy or not life-giving. I want the long-term good for you, and sometimes this may mean a time of testing, and a time of growing. I will certainly heal you, but I cannot promise that I will always cure you. Healing is something that happens inside, and it moves out from there. 'Your sins are forgiven, arise and walk.' You must let me enter into the very core of your being, to every area within you in need of healing. When you look at yourself, or think about yourself, you are aware of things in you that need healing. When I look at you I can see areas in need of healing that you don't even suspect. I take your viewpoint seriously, and I do not at all say that you're wrong. All I'm saying is that I want to broaden the scope of your healing. I want it to work from the inside out. It may surprise you, but the body is the simplest and easiest part to heal! It is much more difficult to heal the inner hurts, the resentments, the unforgiveness, and the guilt. Quite often this is what has contributed to what is wrong with the body. When you have a resentment against somebody, it is as if you were drinking poison, and expecting the other person to die! In other words, you are the one who is being damaged by the resentment. Don't always imagine that the guilt you feel is coming from me! I came to save, not to condemn. If you were to take an inventory of your inner self at this very moment; if you were to spread that out before me; and if we both went through it together, we might find something like the following: regrets, hindsights, resentments, jealousies, angers, unforgiveness, pride, lust, dishonesty, pretence, etc, etc. You see what I mean when I speak of healing beginning from the inside?

Of this you can be certain: I definitely want to be involved in your healing, because that is central to your redemption. It involves redeeming you from bondages, freeing you from slaveries, releasing you from inner darkness. I want to proclaim my victory within your spirit, to set up my kingdom there, and to ensure that you live a life that is really abundant. This inner healing is the greatest miracle of all, and when it happens, we see our bodily ailments in a totally different light. Continue to spend time with me, continue to sit in my presence. This can happen in a room, in a field, or in a car. I am always there when you turn to me. Because of your physical problems, you may have to involve yourself a great deal with doctors, surgery, or medication. All of these things can be good, and can directly effect your health and well-being. Doctors, by their calling, are involved in the healing ministry. Throughout all of this part of your care, however, I want you to remember that I am here in your heart, that I am with you, and that I will never ever abandon you, or leave you on your own. Make sure that prayer is your constant medication, which never changes, even when the doctors change the tablets. Pray for the doctors, so that my Spirit may guide them in their diagnosis. When I ask you to continually pray, I am not implying that you should always be saying prayers. All I ask is that you try to be continually conscious of my presence with you, and within you. You are not alone. I want to travel this journey with you. When you read the gospels you see how I was there, ready to help, when the people were hungry, when the boat was being tossed about in the storm, when they ran out of wine at Cana.

Thank you for sharing your present situation with me.

Thank you for letting me enter into your worries and concerns. Thank you for turning to me, and accepting me as a friend who loves you so much that you are always in my thoughts. When I say that I want to walk this journey with you, I mean that I want you to leave the past to my mercy, the future to my providence, and the present to my love and healing. I am fully present to you now, just as you are, at this very moment. I am the Good Shepherd, and I am concerned when one of the sheep gets tangled in the briars, or falls down a ravine. It is my role to rescue, to save, to come to the aid of the one who cries out to me.

7. I am lonely, Lord

Speak...

God, Father, Son, and Spirit, I feel very much alone at this moment. I feel like a tiny boat out in the middle of the ocean, without oars or a rudder. Oh, I know there are people who are never far away, but at times I experience them as being miles away from me. I don't like being this way, and yet I don't like complaining, or running the risk of wallowing in self-pity. Life hasn't always been like this; indeed, I never thought I'd ever feel so alone in this big world. I turn to you now because I'm sure there is some connection between my feeling of being adrift, and my failure to be fully conscious and aware of your presence within me. To be honest, this is not something that is part of my everyday living. I often confuse you with religion, which most times doesn't do a great deal for me. Even while present at a community celebration in church, I can feel totally alone and not part of anything. I sometimes feel guilty, I must confess, because I seldom seem to turn to you unless I'm looking for something.

Because I don't understand much about how you relate to me, or how best I should pray, I just turn to you and pour out to you exactly how I feel. I want this to be a moment when I can meet you, and really know and experience your presence.

(Take some time out, at this stage, to relax, to sit back, to follow your breath down into your inner being, so that you can begin to open up inside.)

Here I am, Lord. I speak to you in the singular, even though I am thinking of you as being the total Godhead, Father, Son, and Spirit. With what faith I have, I certainly

know that you can do for me what I never could do for myself. I bow before you, and open up all emptiness and loneliness inside. I feel like a shell right now, and a very brittle and
fragile shell at that. I'm not saying that there's nothing inside;
it's just that it's all so stirred up, so much stuff spinning
around, that I can't make head or tail of it. I don't know
where to start, and I feel that I just don't have the mental energy to tackle it.

At this very moment, all I want to do, and indeed all I can
do, is to come before you, just as I am, and talk to you about
it. You can see within me, and you know everything that's
going on there. I like to think that you see much more than I
can see, and that maybe, from your point of view, the picture
may not look so grim. I like to think, and I would want to believe, that you can make some sense out of it all. All I can tell
you is that I'm lonely, I feel very much alone, and at times the
future scares me. If this is how I feel now, what are things
going to be like four or five years from now? Everyday I see
people who seem to be bubbling with life; whose lives seem
to be brimful of activity, and who appear never to have a dull
moment. I can feel totally alone in the most crowded thor-
oughfare, even as I push my way through the crowds.
Because there is life all around me, that makes me suspect
that maybe the problem is within myself. It is from within the
core of my being that my prayer comes, that my cry for help
is spoken. I'm afraid of myself, Lord, because I don't want to
fill this inner vacuum with anything else but you. There were
times when I tried other ways, but they worked only for a
while, and nothing really had changed. Now, with all my
heart, I turn to you. Everything I have ever heard about you
has had to do with love, friendship, goodness, compassion,
and belonging. I need all of that right now, Lord.

Father, the very word speaks of life and of love. You created
me. You know me through and through. You put me together
in my mother's womb. You breathed your Spirit into me, and
gave me life. I am your child, and I would love to have the

heart of a child when I come before you. You clearly see the Inner Child in me that now feels very much alone. I do not believe that that is what you want for me. You gave me life, and you want me to live it to the full. For many many reasons, I seem to have lost my way. I can deal with life so much better when there's something happening. It is much more than just a question of being bored. I don't seem to be going anywhere, and that feeling frightens me. I am also afraid that I might have recourse to any of the many self-medication drugs, to block out the feeling. Somewhere, deep within my soul, there is a spark of hope, and that is what has caused me to turn to you now. I don't understand, but somewhere within, I believe. There is something within that must be of you, because, while not understanding, I feel that you are the only one who can fill the void, who can remove the loneliness. Substances, such as drugs, alcohol, etc, can do that for a while. That was what happened before. This time, however, I want a permanent healing; I want something that will be there tomorrow, and for every tomorrow. I am sick and tired of being sick and tired. I have had enough. Maybe this is what you were waiting for. Maybe, all this time, you were waiting for me to admit defeat, so that you could take over, and do for me what I never could do for myself. Even as I speak to you I am beginning to feel better; the spark of hope is beginning to be fanned into life.

Jesus, it is at a time like this that I think of you as the Good Shepherd. One of your sheep seems to have wandered away from the flock. I don't have any sense of belonging, or of being led. This is probably my own fault, but I know that you are not in the business of blaming, nor do you want me to blame myself. I'm with you now, and that's all that matters to you. I want to have a real sense of belonging, of belonging to you, and to the flock of your community, of your people. I know that I cannot find security outside of myself, in another person, or in possessions, power, or acclaim. That is why I am going within, knowing that you live there, and that you are always there with me, even when I forget, choose to ignore, or become my independent stubborn self. Lord Jesus, Good Shepherd, please stir up within me a deep sense and awareness of your presence, of your love, and your accompaniment in my life. Sometimes I let life close in on me, so that I end up in solitary confinement, with only myself in my own world. I know this is wrong, but it doesn't stop me from doing it. I cannot look to myself for whatever it takes to prevent that happening, so I really really want to entrust this shortcoming to you, asking you to remove it, to stir up within me a whole new enthusiasm for life, to enkindle within me the fires of divine love. Jesus, Redeemer, please free me from the bondage of loneliness and of self. Loosen the chains, and set my heart free to live and to walk with the abundant life you offer. Let me put my hand in yours, let me know your constant touch, so that you can lead me along with a deep consciousness of never being alone.

Spirit, Breath and Power of God, Jesus calls you the Comforter. I know that you are like a gurgling vibrant living spring of water, deep within my being, even when I fill and clutter up the well with garbage, and with my own human cares and worries. With all my heart I pray that you may rise to the surface within me, bringing all that rubbish to the top, to be disposed of in the ocean of God's purifying love. There are times, many times, when the body gets tired, feels unwell, and is experienced as a burden that weighs me down. I want to think of you as the power, the engine, the generator of my inner self. Please set my heart on fire with new hope, and fresh enthusiasm, and burn away all that is not of God. Set my spirit free that I may know your presence and your power. Jesus said that you would never leave us. You are to my inner self what a breath is to my body. Of all the things Jesus said about you, the one that means most to me now is that you would remind us of all that he told us. That is at the heart of my problem. I keep forgetting; I drift along, without any great thought; and it scares me to think of how asleep I can be. I have no doubt that you must clearly see just how much of me is dormant, how much of me is stagnant, how much of me is lifeless. I see your presence as central to my awakening, to my revival, to my survival. Please lift me out of the quicksand, as you fill my soul with the divine helium gas of your breath. Please give me lift-off, allowing me rise above the morass of anxiety, loneliness and fear. Please continue to remind me, to make your presence known, to guide my feet along the pathways of your inspiration and your re-creation. Please help me, lead me, teach me to walk in your power, with a heart that has wings, with a mind that has peace, and with a tongue that whispers my thanks, appreciation, and praise.

Listen...

Thank you, my child, for turning to us in your need. Thank you for acknowledging our presence within you. A prayer like yours means great joy in heaven, and heaven itself comes into your heart. Yes, we are here, we are with you each and every moment of each and every day. Through creation, salvation, and redemption, we can share our life with you, and you can join in sharing your life with us. You are called to full membership in the Trinity, you are called to share in divinity, you are called to live with us and through us. You are never ever alone, because we have chosen your heart as our dwelling, and we are with you always. On a human level, Jesus often felt alone, very much alone, among the throngs. To refresh his spirit, he often slipped away to be alone, because it was at such times that he poured out his heart to me, from his place of exile, and it was at such times that he was least alone. I know it can be difficult for you to understand that being alone and being lonely doesn't mean the same thing. Quite often, you have to go aside, be alone, be still, let the muddy water within settle, and then you will know the presence of the deity within you. Imagine a pearl in muddy water. It is only when the muddy water has settled and become clear that you can see the pearl.

My dear child, this is your Father speaking. If you think of me as a parent, you will have a much more real and accurate awareness of my presence. What parent would want a child to feel lost? Unlike earthly parents, I can watch over you, I can be with you, right there beside you, right there within you at every moment of every day. No, my child, you are not alone. Loneliness can come from choosing to be alone, and this choice can be made in the midst of things, on a busy city street. You have my full attention, and my total love and care at every moment, but nothing happens unless you acknowledge my presence, unless you turn to me, unless you go down into your heart and meet me there. I always love when you come aside for a while to be alone with me. I love when you spend time with me; I love when you have time for me. I created you in love, because I want to share all that is mine with you. I want you to think of me as watching over you at every moment. I am aware of your every thought and deed. I want you to allow me be God, and not try to take on powers, tasks, and burdens that are beyond you. I understand your failings, and I am always ready to raise you up on your feet again, every time you fall. I would love to be given the initiative in your life over all the many things that you turn into human endeavour. I would like to be included in all your plans, hopes, and desires, right from the start, rather than you going ahead on your own getting it wrong, and then turning to me. I will still be there for you, of course, but, as I see things, the loneliness, the isolation, and the alienation, are totally unnecessary. If you could take the focus off yourself, and turn to me; if you could let me be your starting point; if you were fully convinced, beyond all manner of doubt, of my constant and faithful love for you, and put that as being infinitely more important that any love you have to offer me ... that would turn your loneliness around, because your beginning, your point of departure would have changed completely. When you begin with yourself, you are always alone, and always lonely, because I have never created another human being exactly like you. You are unique in the whole history of the human race. It is only when you turn to me that you will be open to meeting the others. I am the source of all human life, and when you are in touch with me, when you are deeply conscious of my presence with you, and within you, then your heart becomes open to fullness and to fellowship. You will never feel alone again...

My friend, this is your friend, Jesus. I came on this earth to join you on your journey. Incarnation is not something that happened once off in Nazareth. That was only the beginning. I continue to become incarnate within the hearts of all those who allow me enter. I stand at the door and knock. If anyone opens the door, I will come in, and I will make my home with that person. Not only will I walk every step with you, but I will guide you on the way, and protect you from the perils and dangers of the journey. I have no trouble understanding your loneliness. Even among my apostles, I often felt totally alone, because they were interested in their own way of doing and thinking, and failed to understand what I tried to teach them. It was because of such times that I always needed to get away on my own, to be alone, so that I could be in touch with my Father. He knew why I was on the earth, he knew what I was about, he understood the love and longings within my heart. I can understand the loneliness that comes from not being understood, appreciated, listened to, or confirmed. You may have heard what is called the loneliness of the long-distance runner, and that is a good description of how I often felt, as the apostles continued to lag behind because of their fear of where they might have to go. I can understand the loneliness that comes from not being wanted, and from not having a sense of belonging. My own most painful loneliness was on the cross, when for a brief moment it seemed that even the Father had abandoned me. I know just how terrifying it can be to feel totally alone.

There is a song, a hymn, called 'You're not alone, my friend, anymore'. I only wish your heart would sing that song. I will never abandon you, I will never leave you in the storm. I will be with you always, even till the end of time. Heaven and earth will pass away before any one of my promises to you will pass away. When you feel alone and lonely, it's usually because there is no one else in your life, and, at this moment, who you are, or what you do, doesn't mean a great deal to anyone. It is a basic human need to know that your life and your work are worth something to somebody. It is scary to find yourself adrift, out at sea in a boat with no sails or no oars. Remember the stories in the gospels when I came to the apostles walking on the water, or when they woke me up, just as the boat began to sink? You are not alone, my friend. I am here with a hand held out to you. Put your hand in mine, and feel my reassuring grip.

There is one point that I wish to make very very clear, so that you are left in no doubt about it. I don't want you to spend all your time with me! I want you to be so aware of my presence within you, that you have the courage and confidence to meet others, and to be with others. Wherever you go, I will go. Like my mother Mary visiting Elizabeth, you are carrying me within you. Be not afraid, you are not alone, my friend, anymore. Remember that I am with you, that I will never lead you where my power and my Spirit will not be there to see you through. Give your full attention to the other person today, remembering that, by doing this, you are doing it to me. I will come to you in many and varied guises this day. You may not easily or readily recognise me! But whoever you meet today, try to remember that that person is me, and whatever you do to her, I will take as being done to me. Because I am living in your heart, I would love you to live with the ideal: I will try to be Christ to others today, and to see Christ in others today.

My child, I am the Spirit, the Breath, and the Power of God. I am the breath that gave life to the clay at the beginning of creation. I am the Spirit that came upon Mary, and that completely changed the hearts of the Apostles at Pentecost. I am that inner energy that vitalises your every word and act. I am to your inner spirit, what your breath is to your body. I am the Comforter in your loneliness. I am that Power Within that goes with you wherever you go. I can understand your loneliness, but my role, among others, is to inspire and remind you. I can fill you with enthusiasm, so that you have a sense of God (*Theos*) within. I am as near to you as the breath that you breathe. I can hover over the waters of your spirit, and bring order out of chaos, and fill all the emptiness within. I can make it that you will never be less alone than when alone. I can be that cloud by day, and the fire by night that accompanied the Hebrews on their journey through the desert; the cloud to shelter from the heat, and the fire to keep away the cold. No, my child, as with the Father and Jesus, I too say that you are not alone, my friend, anymore. Please, let me accompany you in everything you do, in every path you walk, in every word you say...

8. I'm afraid, Lord

Speak...

Lord Jesus, I'm afraid, and fear is something that seems to be part of my life. I have all kinds of fears, from being scared of living to being afraid of dying. I want to tell you about my fears, because no one else could really understand, and, anyhow, I myself don't even understand some of my fears. I experience fear as something that cripples me at times, that bothers me at others, and that seems to lurk within my spirit most times. I cannot always put a name on my fear. Sometimes it's nothing more than shyness; at other times it feels like a knot in my stomach that halts me in my tracks, and prevents me enjoying the day I have been given for living, or the experience I am offered to enjoy.

I'm afraid of change, not sure what is lurking around the next corner. I'm afraid of making decisions, of making commitments, or of letting go of control. I'm afraid of pain, of sickness, and I'm always afraid that I'll break down, crack up, or lose all sense of security. I find it difficult to relax, to throw discretion to the winds, or to take risks. This is what gives me a feeling that I'm afraid to really live, to give life my best shot. I'm afraid of what others might think of me, of what others might say about me, of how others might see me. There are times when I feel like a rabbit caught in the headlights of an on-coming car, or a baby being immersed in a bath, or a child passing a graveyard at night on a lonely country road. The fear seems to cling to me, to haunt, to mock me. What makes it worse is that I can't speak to others about a lot of my fears, for fear of what they might think of me. It is as if the fear is self-perpetuating, continually regenerating itself. If I run, it comes with me; if I hide, it is waiting for me; if I try to ignore it, it seems to bully me into reminding me of its presence.

I'm afraid of myself, because of my weaknesses. There are times when I cannot trust myself at all; when, being alone with myself, I feel that I'm in unhealthy and dangerous company. There are times when I experience my own inner personal demons, and that scares me. I am afraid of the unknown, and I'm often afraid to think too deeply, because I'm afraid of my thoughts, which can be a very real source of my fears. I often experience the war that rages within me, and I'm afraid of losing the battle. I'm afraid to take on the demons, to name them for what they are, and to expose them to the light of love and of understanding. Sometimes I'm even afraid of love, because this might cause me to lose control, and it might cost me something. I can be afraid of the cost of being open and honest, and afraid of what I might have to surrender if I drop the mask, or lower my guard.

I'm afraid of authority in every form. The very presence of an authority figure puts me in a state of full alert. My fear expresses itself in many forms at such times. I choose my words, I assume a mentality of defence, and I feign total agreement with all that is being said. I experience my fear as being moral cowardice, and my behaviour as being subservient. I hate this in myself, and that feeling makes things worse. I experience myself as being dishonest and inauthentic, when I allow my fear influence my opinions, my ideas, and my beliefs. I don't ever want to be aggressive, but I certainly don't want to be a moral coward. This fear of authority often extends to people who have no authority over me. I believe them to be superior to me, so I give them an authority that does not belong to them.

Lord, I'm afraid of failure, I'm afraid of being seen as a loser. I have experienced so much of my own brokenness that I'm afraid to take risks, I'm afraid to step out and take control of situations. I'm afraid of choices, and I'm happier when someone else makes the choice for me. I opt out of situations because of my fears, and this brings yet more fear, when I consider the price I am paying through the loss of integrity, and of wholesome living. I'm afraid of time, because it just keeps passing by regardless, and I have no control over it. As each second passes, I am aware that it will never ever return. I fear the consequences of the waste of time, and I can get uncomfortable to find time on my hands. I like to work within schedules, and I like to meet others' expectations of me. I like to be liked, and I shudder at the thought of rejection and scorn. I'm always afraid of being different, and this fear often leads me into conformity, when I really don't want to conform.

Lord, I'm afraid of my emotions; I'm afraid of my moods. When I waken up in the morning, I'm just not sure how I'm going to feel today. There are days when I seem to hit an air-pocket, go into some sort of nose-dive, and life goes into a spin. There are days when I just want to go back to bed, cover my head, and tell the whole world where to go. Something happens inside that triggers off a sense of gloom and doom, and I feel I just don't want to face the world. It becomes a question of me and them. I don't feel at one with the human race; I don't feel at one with myself. I experience a sense of dis-ease, I become restless, and I can't seem to settle. I know it is fear of some kind, though I cannot put a name on it. It seems as if some part of my inner self is unable to come out, and to meet the world today. Because this appears to be some kind of hiding, that is why I suspect the presence of fear. As a child, I was terrified of thunder and lightening. I monitored the clouds as they gathered and darkened, and I knew it was getting to the time to pull the curtains. That is something like what I experience today. A dark cloud has descended, and I just want to pull the curtains. Leave me alone; don't try to talk me out of it. It is not a question that *I* have this fear and this sense of gloom and doom, but *it* seems to have *me*. I feel hopeless, helpless, and powerless. This depression can descend out of the bluest sky, without warning and, even when not present, I am afraid it may be about to descend, to blot out the sunshine I am enjoying.

I'm afraid of loneliness, Lord. I'm afraid of those empty hollow hours, when nothing is happening and there is no one around but myself to cause things to happen. I can become frozen into inactivity, when I just sit with my fears and hope they go away. When they have gone away, I'm afraid they will return. I'm afraid of what I might do at such times. I'm afraid of addiction. I'm afraid to abdicate control to some monster that might get beyond control. I can become fearful, full of fear. I feel caught on some sort of merry-go-round, and I develop a fear of fear itself. If it's not present now, then it's just around the next corner waiting to pounce. Lord, no wonder I turn to you now, and cry out to you. Quite often, in the past, I allowed the fear develop into panic before I called to you. Today I want to do something entirely different. I want to come to you with each and every fear I have. I want to name them, to acknowledge them, to share them with you, and to ask you to take them all away from me. I have many individual fears, like dogs, darkness, flying, water, death, etc, and, while including all my fears, whatever they are, what I pray for now is the removal of fear itself from my life.

I'm afraid of responsibility, Lord, because that exposes me to failure. I'm afraid to have to take the blame when things go wrong. I feel more secure within the flock than to have to assume leadership, to express initiative. I'm afraid to stand up and be counted on certain issues, because that might cause others not to like me. In today's world, where there is so much debate on controversial issues, I often remain silent, lest my opinion may prove unpopular, and I might draw fire from those around me. I experience how fear can make a coward out of me, and how such cowardice can make me dishonest. I have gone along with suggestions with which I disagreed, because I was afraid to stand up and be counted.

Lord, I'm afraid of fear itself. It can grip me in its control, and make me powerless. It can destroy a great deal of my potential, and greatly limit my ability to be effective. In my earlier days, I was taught to fear God. I didn't understand that to be anything different from the fear I would have towards evil or danger. My religion had a great deal of fear in it. I often performed religious duties out of a fear of neglecting them. I often acted out of fear, rather than love. My obedience, my behaviour, my participation in community celebrations, were often motivated by a sense of obligation, rather than voluntary and spontaneous service. Fear of neglect, and the results of such neglect, in the immediate and in the long-term, were often my motivating forces. The rules, regulations, and laws always generated fear in me. There was a servility about my actions that was not very life-giving or inspiring.

Lord, I'm afraid of the future. It stretches like a long dark tunnel up in front of me, and I don't know what it holds. It can distract me from living and enjoying the now. Life seems to just move ahead relentlessly, with some sort of preconditioned force, and I experience my own powerlessness to control it. The ageing process continues and, with each day, I continue to experience evidence of that. I sometimes experience myself as walking into the unknown, like someone on safari in the midst of a jungle. I don't know what's going to happen next. I know that this is certainly not the way you want me to live my life, and that is why I turn to you now. Friends, relatives, associates have died on either side of my age, and I often wonder how or when my turn will come. This is one fear that I cannot dwell on, because it has the potential to cripple the rest of my life. I often question, and sometimes fear entering the unknown at the point of death. I fear that which I don't know, cannot understand, or am unable to control.

Yes, indeed, Lord, fear is very much part of my life, and it has the potential to be very destructive. There are times when I can clearly see just how crazy and unrealistic my fears can be. I try to reason with myself, to work things out logically in my head, to be as objective as possible. This works for a while, but then, as if out of the blue, that familiar gut-feeling returns, and in no time at all I'm in knots of fear. It is as if this fear of fear is lurking just under the surface, waiting for the right moment. I can't go on this way. There has to be something better, there has to be a better way. That is why, Lord, I'm bringing the whole lot to you today, dumping the lot at your feet, and asking 'Please take away my fears. Please set me free from fear. Please enter my heart and my inner spirit, with a whip of cords, if needed, and rid the temple of my heart of everything that is not of you. Lord, from this day, from this moment, I ask you, please, to remove fear of every kind from my life...'

Listen...

Thank you, thank you, my dear dear friend; thank you for coming to me, and asking to rid your heart and your life of fear. The word fear is mentioned again and again in the gospels. The first time the word appears in the Bible is immediately after Adam and Eve fell for the lie in the Garden. 'They hid, because they were afraid.' That is the first mention of the word 'fear' in the whole story of creation and redemption. Satan is the father of lies, and he has been a liar right from the very beginning. Part of his technique is to put fear where there is nothing to fear. To do so is to deceive, to tell a lie. I came to set you free, so that, in the words of Zachary, the father of John the Baptist, 'free from fear, and saved from the hands of your foes, you might serve the Lord in holiness and justice all the days of your life'. Fear is an enemy, it is part of the technique for bringing dis-ease into the soul, and making you unhealthy. 'Fear not. Be not afraid. Why are you fearful, you of little faith?' The gospels are littered with such phrases. It would be worth your while sometime to check this recurring theme throughout the gospels, so that you might all the more be convinced how central to my mission of salvation and redemption is the eradication of fear from the human heart. I want to fill you with my love, and love and fear cannot co-exist in the same heart. In his first letter, St John summarises this whole question in words that you should write

out, reflect on, and even memorise. 'God is love, and all who
live in love live in God, and God lives in them ... So we will
not be afraid on the day of Judgement, but we can face him
with confidence ... Such love has no fear, because perfect love
expels all fear. If we are afraid, it is for fear of judgement, and
this shows that his love has not yet been perfected in us.'

Thank you for coming to me with all your fears. Of course,
I want to rid you of those fears. I came that you should have
life, and have it more abundantly. You cannot have full life,
and be riddled with fear at the same time. Fear, in itself, is not
an evil. It is part of the instincts of human nature, and is
greatly expanded because of original sin. My own mother,
who was without original sin, was told by the angel 'Be not
afraid', because fear is the most natural reaction to something
unusual and unexpected happening. It is a painful emotion
caused by impending danger or evil. My mother was not
afraid in that sense. Rather was it a case of fright, which is a
natural human reaction to certain sudden events. Fear is
more than just fright, however. It is a disease of the soul; it is
something that usurps a place that is created for love. It is an
intruder into the temple of love that is created to be a home
for divinity, a place where the kingdom is to be established.
Fear can make cowards of people, but fear itself is a coward.
It is a bully, that runs when confronted with the truth which
exposes it as the impostor it really is.

My dear dear friend, I know your fears. I watched your
battles and struggles with fears for some time now. I so much
longed to intervene, but I had to wait till you invited me. I
longed to enter your house, like so many houses in the gospel
stories _ the houses of Jairus, Zacchaeus, Peter's mother-in-
law, or the house where the man was lowered on the stretcher.
Once the door was opened to me, and I was invited to enter, I
then had the freedom to work the miracle. It may seem
strange to you to hear that there are very definite conditions
that limit my power to do good in a soul, or to work a miracle
in a situation. I will never ever intrude into a human heart, or

a human situation. On one occasion, I returned to Nazareth and I could not work any miracles there because they didn't want me to be there. I am extremely sensitive to the free-will of the people concerned. I'm sure you yourself have come across people whom you couldn't help because they would not accept your help. It is the same with me. If you cry out to me, I will respond immediately.

There is one point I want to make absolutely clear. I have overcome the enemy, I have the victory over this world, and all its evils. Full authority is given to me in heaven and on earth. When you invite me into your heart, please remember that I bring all that power and victory with me, and I want to declare and proclaim that victory in you. In other words, it's not simply a question of me coming into your heart; rather is it a question that I bring that power and victory with me, to establish and to effect that victory within you. I came to establish the kingdom of God, and I want that kingdom to be within the hearts of my people. That kingdom is based on love, not fear. Where my kingdom is established there is no fear. The spirit of fear is overcome and expelled. When I establish my kingdom, I put all the enemies there under my feet, and I proclaim the victory. I am the same yesterday, today, and always. The victory I establish and proclaim is an eternal victory, and when I overcome and expel fear, it is gone for all time. In your prayer, you opened the doors, and exposed all your fears. I have always been aware of them, and I have always been willing to enter in, and rid your heart of everything that is not of me. Thank you for inviting me into your heart.

I walked this earth just like you do now. I met many many people each and every day. I encountered fears of all descriptions. My constant word was 'Fear not, I am with you'. Where I am there is no fear, there is nothing to fear. When I encountered Satan, he was filled with fear, and he had every reason to be afraid. Satan is a bully, and he thrives on fear, intimidation, confusion, and conflict. I exposed him for the liar that he is, and I told him that his days were numbered. It is my role, as the Good Shepherd, to reassure my flock, to protect them, and to keep them safe from everything that might harm them, or cause them to be afraid. I declared my willingness to die for my flock, rather than let the marauders attack them, and fill them with fear. I was always ready to reassure the apostles that I was near, and they had nothing to fear. I came to them on the waters when their boat was being buffeted by the storm. At the Last Supper I assured them again and again that they had nothing to fear, even after I left them. I asked them to remain in my love, and I assured them that the evil one had no power over them. Their names were registered as citizens of heaven and, having prepared a place for them, I would return to bring them safely home, so that where I am they always will be. I promised to send them the Holy Spirit, the Comforter, who would never leave them. One of the first effects of Pentecost was that the apostles came bounding out of that Upper Room, completely fearless, and free to be my witnesses. They had locked themselves in that room because of fear. Now they were free from fear, and in their preaching and their writing they declared that one of the fruits of re-demption is freedom from fear.

I see fears in you that I know you have inherited. I now want to go back down the corridor of time, to where those fears began, and to wither them at the roots. Those fears are not from me, and I want to set you free. I want to loosen the grip that fear has established in your heart and soul, and to replace that with peace and love. I want to heal all the scars of mind and of memory, so that you can leave the past totally to me, and have nothing to fear from that past. There is nothing you can do that will change yesterday, which went away at midnight and will never return. Only I can change, redeem, heal, and free your past. Please leave all of that with me, and let me take care of it. If you accept me as your personal Saviour, then I will take full control of anything in the past than needs healing, forgiveness, or freedom from bondage. If you imagine your past being a room, then please come out of that room and leave me in charge, so that I can redeem and reclaim it totally.

I see fears in you that have to do with your health, both physical and mental. Just pause and think for a moment. If you let me into your heart, if you let me take over, if you turn all those fears over to me, surely you must expect something very definite and very dramatic to happen. I don't want you to have those fears. If it were my will that you should have these illnesses, then, you can be sure, you would have what it takes to grow through them, and to become a better person because of them. When they fill you with fear, surely they are not from me. If they are not from me, then surely I want to remove them. I died for you. You are my very special friend, and I am your forever friend. It is certainly not my wish that you have fears that are not for your growth or for your good. When I make my home in your heart, do you seriously believe that I will allow those fears to remain in my presence? All I ask is that you let me be Lord in your heart, that you put me in charge of all those things that are beyond your power to control. Don't forget, if you were the only person on this planet, I still would have come to redeem you, and to set you free. I work and think in a very personal way, and so I am able to give you my full attention at every moment of every day. Again and again I have assured you that I would never abandon you, or leave you in the storm. I am with you always, and I will be with you until the end of time, until you are back with my Father, free from fear, free at last.

I see your fear of others, whether it be those in authority, those with a decision-making role in your life, or simply those whom you consider can harm or hurt you. Please remember where all authority and power lies. It is within your heart, and you need never give another human being power over you. There are chores, tasks, and undertakings that are part of your everyday life. I want to be part of every single one of these, and I want you to know that I will be there with you, and for you, every step of the way. Look inwards, before you look outwards. The only real security in your life is within yourself, and don't ever seek security in anything or in anyone but me. Remember that I live within the heart of the other person also, and I will never permit anything happen that, together, we will be unable to handle. I will never lead you where my grace and my Spirit will not be there to see you through.

I am very conscious of your fears about the future. The future is something that is totally unknown to you, but it is not unknown to me. You need never fear what the future holds, if you allow me hold the future. Your future is in safe hands, if you leave it in my care. 'Who do you say that I am?' is one of the most important questions I have ever asked. If you allow me take over that room of your past, then you are accepting me as your Saviour. If you entrust to me that room of your future, then you are putting me in charge, and allowing me be Lord. And that leaves today, where I ask you to accept me as God, and stop trying to do things, control things, arrange things that only God can do. In a very real way, you have to stop playing God! I will become God in your life the very moment you step out of the way, and let me be God, for whom nothing is impossible.

I now want to bless you. I place my hand upon your head. I use my power, my victory, and my authority, and I bind within you all the fears, the anxieties, the phobias, and the worries. I breathe my Spirit into you, yet again, to fill every corner of your heart, and I entrust to the Spirit the task of reminding you, again, again, and again, that you have no reason to be afraid, because I am with you; the Father is with you; the Spirit lives in you. You are a citadel, a stronghold of God, and nothing, but nothing, can harm you.

(If you suffer from a fear of death, please reflect on the second part of Chapter 12).

9. I'm an alcoholic, Lord

(This prayer can be used for any and every form of addiction, by replacing the word 'alcohol' with whatever word applies.)

God, Higher Power, Power greater than myself, I cry out to you. I feel like someone who has ventured out on a journey, and I have ended up in a swamp. The more I struggle to free myself, the more aware I am of sinking. I am caught in the nets of an addiction. I never set out to be this way. I never wanted to be an alcoholic. It just seems to have crept up on me, and caught me totally unawares. Oh, I know that I was warned, and reminded by others, but I thought that I was the one to know and to decide whether I was in control or not. I didn't know that part of the disease is its ability to deny its own existence. I admit that it has bothered me, and indeed burdened me for many years now, but I had every intention of taking control of the situation and correcting what was amiss. My behaviour has brought misery to myself and to those around me. I have been riddled with guilt, filled with remorse, and very unhappy with what was happening. I would, of course, stop, but the right time just didn't seem to have arrived. I definitely would stop some day, but I wasn't ready just yet. This has been going on for some time now. Even when I stopped, I never felt stopped, and I was always waiting for the next slip, and off I went again.

In my head, I want to be sober, to be clean, but there is something deep down within the core of my being, and I often imagine getting a JCB, going down inside there and shifting it, whatever it is. Sometimes I think of it as a demon, and, at other times, it is like some bottomless abyss that is impossible to fill. There never seems to be enough alcohol. Even as I drink, my mind is planning how, where, and when the next drink is going to come from. I experience myself in a very frightening grip of something that I just cannot shake off, something that continues to dog my steps, to trip me up, to pull me down. There are times when I cry out for help, but I just cannot accept the help of those around me. They couldn't possibly understand what it's like. I'm afraid, genuinely afraid, of where all this may lead me. I know I should and must do something about it, and I dread that I'll hit skid row before I'm ready to move. My whole life is one long string of failures, of broken promises, of unfulfilled resolves.

Lord, I feel that something like alcohol, which had been a friend for so long, is now turning on me, and is out to destroy me. And I honestly believe that it has the power to destroy me, and all those I hold dear. It seems to have a grip on me that I cannot shake off. I am filled with anger whenever I reflect on what is happening to me. Those thoughts are too hurtful, so I drink again to block the thinking, or to numb the pain. At my better moments I see all of this as total insanity, where I keep repeating the same pattern, and continue to hope for a different result. I'm going around in circles, even when I'm not drinking, because I always seem to end up in the same place, in the same state as before. I experience a quiet desperation that is getting me nowhere, because my pattern of behaviour continues to be the same. My guilt causes me to be irritated by the complaints or the advice of others. In my better moments, I know they are right, and I intend taking care of this situation when I know the time is right. But not just yet...

Lord, I'm sick and tired of being sick and tired. Every waking day, after the previous night's indulgence, fills me with self-disgust, self-loathing, and a real stubborn resolve, that says 'Never again'. That resolve lasts until the first opportunity arises, and off I go again. I try desperately to hold this demon at bay. I compare myself to others I know, and they are so much worse than I am, which convinces me that I may not be so bad after all. I go for short periods without a drink, and I use this as evidence that I can stop when I want to. All my so-called 'narrow-scrapes' are seen as something that could have been worse and, therefore, don't appear to be very serious. I continue to defend the indefensible, to justify the injustice, and to rationalise the insanity. There is a constant battle going on in my head, and sometimes I feel like I am totally defeated. The feeling doesn't last too long, once I get the glass back in my hand. Part of me actually hates alcohol for what I know and see it is doing to me, but my alcoholic mind takes over, and I am free to drink again. It is as if this demon is prepared to fight to the death for its own survival. I experience a restlessness within, and an inability to apply myself totally to any one task for any great length of time. It is as if I have some sort of runaway engine inside, and I am no longer at the controls. I pray sometimes but, even then, my guilt drains the life out of my prayers. How can I ask you to remove something that I really don't want to surrender? This makes me feel even a greater hypocrite, so I stop praying. What's the point? In my saner and better moments, I know rightly what I ought to do and, somehow, I feel that the first step towards recovery must begin from within myself.

I don't find it easy to admit to powerlessness. I have never found it easy to admit defeat. There is pride, stubbornness, and some sort of a crazy independent streak within, that refuses to concede that I might be wrong, and that others might be right. I argue, rationalise, and justify and, when that fails, I get angry. I feel isolated and misunderstood, which is often as good a reason as any for another drink. I have never been short of reasons for drinking, of course, but I have gone through some strange mental gymnastics to justify my actions. I have been so successful at this, at times, that I genuinely believed that I was right. I discovered a great reserve of cunning and guile, and I have used this to great advantage.

This has lead me into all kinds of deviousness and deception. I had a sense of inner erosion, as one ideal, or one moral standard after another began to crumble in the dust. My conscience haunted me for a while but, after sufficient alcohol, I noticed it bothered me less and less. It was as if I was giving up on myself, without being aware of it.

I was often conscious of being at full stretch within, trying to preserve my life style, to protect my supply. It was as if something within was about to snap. I knew I just couldn't keep going, that something had to give. I began to notice how family and friends began to change in their attitudes and in their dealings with me. I saw reflected in their looks the very feelings I was experiencing within. I saw that they had begun to realise what I myself had dreaded, and what, all along, I began to see in myself. I became uncomfortable in the company of those who held up that mirror to me, and I was driven more and more into isolation. With all the camaraderie, and all the celebration that appears to go with drink, I began to feel very much alone. I even began to feel uncomfortable in my own company. I drank secretly to fill the empty moments, or to avoid dwelling on reality, as I feared it to be. I can never claim that anyone ever poured alcohol down my throat, and yet I could not see that my situation was entirely of my own making. I was surrounded by people and situations that would drive anyone to drink! Or so I thought. I might even be prepared to concede that alcohol was destroying me and my life, but I stopped short of holding myself responsible for drinking the alcohol in the first place.

Right here, right now, I am experiencing defeat; I feel that I'm beaten. I may not yet be ready to admit that to others but, at least, I can do that to myself. As I speak, I am very conscious these words are being addressed to myself, because I am not ready yet to turn completely in the direction of God. I'm afraid of what this might entail, of what I might be asked to do. My drinking has greatly damaged my awareness of God, or my relationship with him. Most of the times I just didn't want to know. Anything or anybody that might come between me and alcohol was pushed to one side. Right now, however, I feel desperately in need of a Higher Power, of a Power greater than myself. I'm afraid of my head, which has played such tricks on me in the past, so I want this cry for help to come from my heart. I don't know how best to do this. I only know how to get alcohol, how to drink alcohol, and how to ensure the next drink. I know very little about a Higher Power, beyond the fact that, somewhere within, I just know that you're there. (Now, at least, and at last, I'm speaking to you!) If you're not there, I'm really in trouble, because I would lose hope completely, and that terrifies me. That is why I cry out to you, asking you to show yourself, to reveal yourself, to let me know that you're there. I feel like someone sinking in quicksand, and I have both hands in the air, crying for someone to grab them, and stop me sinking any further.

I fall on my knees, in blind faith, and I pray: Higher Power, God, please please help me, please reach out a hand to rescue me. My situation is desperate, my life is out of control, and I can no longer manage it. I have gone into a nose-dive, into a tail-spin, and I'm headed for disaster. Please please help me, because I can no longer help myself. I'm 'bet', I've run out of steam, out of excuses, out of hiding places. I've had enough, and if there's any way back, please take me by the hand, and bring me back. I don't care what human resources you use, whether that be treatment, recovery programme, counselling, or whatever. I feel I have no choice but to surrender, and to hand over the steering wheel before I drive over the cliff. Somewhere within my being, I feel that I have called out just in time, and I believe that it's not too late for you. I ask you, please, to keep me out of my head, to keep me down in my heart. I don't want to understand, I don't want any explanations, I don't want any great insights. All I ask is the knowledge that you are taking over, and that I can experience your action in my life. I am quite happy to begin with the experience, and let the understanding come later. Once I can feel your presence, when I become aware that the nightmare is over, that I have made contact with a Power greater than myself, then, and only then, can I begin to relax, and breathe deeply once again. God, Higher Power, I'm riddled with fears because of the horrors of the past, but I have no choice now but to surrender and hand everything over to you. I don't know how you can rescue me, and I don't want to know.

If you are the God who created me, then I believe that you can re-create me. I feel that nothing less than total re-creation and rebirth can resolve my situation, can revive my life, can restore my sanity. Somewhere within my being, without understanding it, I feel that, in answer to my cry for help, you have thrown the door of my cell wide open, and you are inviting me to come out into freedom, into the light. I want to do that, right here, right now. I want to live this moment fully, because I'm afraid of the ghosts of the past, and the demons of the future. I step out, and place my hand in yours right now, and I feel your reassuring grip. Please don't ever let go of that grip, even when I try to pull away from you. I feel like someone who has had a miraculous escape from a shipwreck, and I have no desire to return to the wreck or to the raging storm. While I have graduated through the stages of loving alcohol, to hating alcohol, I am now at a stage where I am terrified of alcohol. Please, please, please, reach out a hand, and rescue me from the clutches of this demon ...

Listen...
My dear dear child. Not only do I take you by the hand, but I draw you close to me, and throw both arms around you. Yes, indeed, you have been saved from a shipwreck, and that's all that matters. You were nearly gone, and unless you called out to me, there was nothing I could do to save you. It is never a question of will-power. If you don't have the will, there's no point in me giving you the power. I have been waiting and watching. I heard the prayers of your loved ones, but I waited

for a response from you. You may find this difficult to understand, but to admit that you are totally beaten is a great victory, rather than a defeat. It is the victory of truth over lies, the victory of humility over pride, the victory of life over death. Pride can be very destructive, and so very very devious. From the fall of Lucifer, to the Fall in the Garden, to this very day, pride has left a trail of death and destruction wherever it existed.

It is not easy to be totally honest, and to admit defeat. It is not easy to admit to powerlessness, and to an inability to manage life. Such things are totally against the inbuilt selfishness that is part of being human. It is not possible for human beings to lift themselves out of the quicksand of their own selfishness. That is why you refer to me, quite rightly, as the Higher Power, because it does take a power greater than yourself to lift you to a higher plain, where you can experience a life beyond your wildest dreams, and indeed beyond your greatest potential. It is never too late for me, and your call came in time, before you went over the waterfall. My hand was always held out to you, but you were neither ready nor willing to grasp it. Alcohol, like any other element of nature, is something that is good in itself, when used properly. It has, however, the potential to totally destroy if allowed get out of control and generate a dependency. It feeds into what is weakest in human nature, which can be uncomfortable with reality and with the ordinary humdrum existence of human living. Human nature is something that is very fragile, very frail, and very easily derailed. There are drives, impulses, emotions, compulsions, and appetites that can so easily get out of control. The problem with many of these is that they are so much part of you that you cannot see them. Alcoholism is the one disease that tries everything to deny its own existence, and if you identify it as the destructive force it is, it will do everything to preserve its existence.

Somewhere within you is the hope and prayer that I can rescue you from this insanity. It is clearly obvious that you yourself are powerless and, after trying everything within your power, you now turn to me. That is good, even if you had come to me earlier I could have saved you a great deal of pain and destruction. Better late than never and, as I said before, it's never too late for me. Letting me take over is really very simple but, for you, it's not going to be easy. Long years of living in a certain way make it more difficult to change. Bad habits die slowly, and some bad habits die much slower than others. Alcoholism is a case of self-will run riot, and so it is not easy to turn around and hand your will over to the care of someone else, even me. You have accepted that your life had become totally unmanageable, and it goes against the grain to have to surrender and let someone else run your life. What I mean here is that any worthwhile change has to be basic, ruthless, and total. If you are honest, and I believe you are, you must admit that all the old ways of doing things must end, that a whole new way of living must be grasped. It is something like a heart, liver, and kidney transplant, where the old must be removed entirely, or it will continue to raise its ugly head. Remember that you deal with alcohol … cunning, baffling, powerful, and very very patient. There must be no going back; therefore, together, we will have to do something about the past. There is no plan for the future either, because, like many another person, how can you claim or be sure of having a future? One heart attack, and your future is gone. The only way to handle this is to develop a way of living in the NOW, with definite guidelines for living today, and with decisions that are meant for today, and today only.

For the present, I ask you, please, to entrust all the wreckage of the past to me. The burden is too much for you to carry. I'm not going to dispose of it, at least yet, because there are too many precious lessons to be learned from it. One thing is certain: nothing you can do will change one moment of the past, so you might as well not bother trying to go back down that road. The past has value in one area only, i.e. for the lessons it has taught you. I want to go through that past with you, day by day, blow by blow, and when you think it has convinced you of the insanity and the irresponsibility of your behaviour, then we can get rid of it for all time. The past is too valuable to be dismissed lightly because of the lessons it can teach us. Remembering what things were like is a very important part of your recovery. The only real value the past has are the lessons it has taught you. You would be a very wise person today if you learned every lesson life has taught you. Compassion is very much part of the life of a Christian, and that can only come from your own brokenness, turmoil, and hurts.

You now have to consider a whole new way of living. This is more than just a question of what to do now with the time and money you have on your hands! This is deadly serious, and your life depends on it. You are sick. You have a disease. Others can drink and not end up like you, simply because they don't have your disease. Some people are blind, and can never see; others are in wheelchairs, and can never walk. Some people can run marathons, while others would collapse and die after the first twenty yards. Please, please, be open to accept reality in your life, however painful or humiliating it may seem. You are an alcoholic; you have a very real allergy to alcohol, and to continue using it will most certainly kill you. It matters little how or why you have become an alcoholic, no more than it matters much to the man dying of a heart attack to be told why his heart is damaged. This is a time for action, and there is no time for arguments, explanations, or reflections. You have a killer disease, and your recovery must begin right now, because tomorrow could be too late. Your alcoholism will try to concentrate on the terror of never being able to drink again, and it can blind you to the thousands of good things you will be able to do, when your life is free from alcohol. You went to great lengths to get the drink, to have time and money for the drink, to protect your supply for the next drink. In recovery, you also have to do things. I certainly will walk every step with you, and I will guide your steps into sobriety, but you have to take and make those steps, because I cannot do them for you. You are the alcoholic, not me!

You are sick and, when you are sick, you should go to a doctor. That's what you should do now. Tell him what you told me, and listen to what he has to say. He cannot make you sober, nor can he solve your problem, but he can point you to the next logical step towards complete recovery. Your condition is spiritual, emotional, mental, as well as physical, so no tablets from a doctor can cure it. Remember your journey into alcoholism? Maybe it was slow, gradual, step by step, day by day. Your road back, your path to recovery, will be something the same. You suffer from a sickness that is unique, because it can be halted, but never cured. It is called alcoholism, and it never becomes alcoholwasm! It is a disease you will carry within you till the day you die, and with just one drink, it will flare up again like a forest fire, and will surely destroy what is left of your life. It is like someone with malaria. For the rest of their lives, without any warning, the malaria will continue to flare up, after long periods of remission. You are an alcoholic, and you always will be an alcoholic. The extraordinary difference is that the alcoholic, without alcohol, has the capacity to lead a life that is fuller, happier, and more fruitful than those who do not have that disease. This is a strange phenomenon, and it results from the gratitude for a second chance at life, from a deep awareness of one's own frailty, and from developing a way of living that gives order and direction to a life that was completely out of control.

I'm going to say something to you now that is very very important : You have a disease, and removing alcohol from the formula will not solve it. As I've just said, it's like someone returning from Africa where the malaria was contracted. For the rest of their lives, no matter where they live, they will always have malaria. The mosquitoes are no longer around, but the harm has been done. To the day you die, you will always be an alcoholic, even if you never touch another drop of alcohol. You need a programme of recovery, something that will continue to be part of every single day. The roots and the causes of your disease continue to be present, and always will be. I now offer you a gift, which you are totally free to accept or reject. I offer you sobriety, and freedom from the compulsion to ever drink again. The programme for living this is already well in place, but you must want what I offer, and be prepared to do what it takes to experience that gift. I cannot force you, compel you, or threaten you. The decision is entirely up to you. I will give you what it takes, and I will walk every step of the road with you, but you must be prepared to do certain things. You must be prepared to turn your will and your life over to me, and to let me guide your feet into the ways of life, peace, and happiness; into a life beyond your wildest dreams.

(Think about this for a while, because it could be one of the most important moments and decisions of your whole life.)

Because you are sick you may need to spend some time in hospital to give your system a chance to recover. Let your doctor be the judge of that. Then you will become part of a recovery programme called Alcoholics Anonymous (AA). If you are prepared to take this step, to listen to what you hear there, and to do what you're told there, then you need never drink again. If you have a genuine desire to stop drinking, then you will follow my directions. If not, then there is nothing I can do for you, because you have chosen to continue your path towards self-destruction and death. I certainly don't want you to turn your back on this offer, because it is life or death. In your own heart, I believe that you don't want to reject it, even if you experience a fear of what all this might entail. Give me your fears, your doubts, your worries, and anxieties, and just trust me to point you in the right direction. At no stage have I said that you are never to drink again. All I said was that you need never drink again, you will never need a drink again.

This method works only one day at a time. I am totally a

God of now. My help is available to you now, right here, right now. If you trust me, you will not have to take up that first drink today. That is my offer, that is my promise. That is the thinking and the type of living towards which I am guiding you. You will find all of that, and so much much more, if you take AA seriously, and are prepared to follow that programme. This programme has come from me, just as much as any church or religious denomination on this earth. It is a spiritual programme, but it has nothing to do with any particular church, denomination, sect, creed, or religion. The only requirement for membership is the desire to stop drinking. Please, please accept the gift that is offered. Come out into freedom from the slavery of this deadly disease. Come out into life, a life beyond your wildest dreams. Remember, in this prayer, you are the one who came to me! I am answering your prayer, I am responding to your cry. Come on, let us travel the path together…

10. I'm depressed, Lord

Speak...
Lord God, Father, Mother, please reach down and lift me out
of this dark hole of depression. I am surrounded by darkness
on every side, and I can see no way out of it. It is like a dark
thunder cloud, or a heavy black fog that has come down
upon me, and I cannot see the road ahead. I feel drained,
empty, useless, hopeless, and helpless. I just feel like going to
bed, covering my head, and I don't want to face the world
again. This is something that happens to me from time to
time, and it frightens me. I feel so powerless, and unable to
do anything about it. It feels as if something has died within
me, that the lights have gone out, and the curtains drawn. I
have a profound sense of loneliness, because no one else
could possibly understand how I feel. I would be much better
if both legs were in plaster, because then, at least, there would
be some external sign that something had happened to me.
But with this depression, I feel cut off from the world, I have
no interest in anything, and I feel that no one has any interest
in me. My own sense of hopelessness is reflected in the faces
of my friends. They don't know what to say, and, when they
try to say something, it is never really helpful. I do not blame
them, of course, but I feel that I'd be better off if they just left
me alone. They cannot enter my world, and I cannot enter
theirs. I feel so bad, because it might appear that I am wallowing in self-pity, or voluntarily locked up in my own little
world.

This awful feeling just fills me with fear, and I dread what
the outcome will be. Sometimes I just don't want to go on liv-

ing, and I hang in there in quiet desperation. All that keeps me going is the hope that it will pass, as it has before, and tomorrow, the sun will come out again. I have a sense of some heavy leaden weight within the pit of my stomach, and I cannot motivate myself to get up and go. The feeling that nothing is happening, that I'm stuck in a state of inactivity, that there is no light at the end of the tunnel, ...all this is really scary. What makes it worse is that I'm afraid to be in touch with my feelings, and I just wish I could go to sleep until the cloud passes, when I could waken up to see the sun again. I don't believe, Lord, that it is your will that I should be in such a dark hole, and that my life should be so lifeless. That is why I cry out to you: Please, please reach down, reach out, take me by the hand, and lift me out of the dungeon. 'It is not good for man/woman to be alone.' Lord, I feel totally alone, totally abandoned. I often seriously query your part in all this. I'm sure you know, and I'm sure you care, but there are so many times when I see no evidence of that. Maybe the very fact that I'm crying out to you now is, in itself, a positive sign, a sign of hope. If I'm honest, I must confess that I turn to you, because I don't know where else to turn. I don't want a life that is dependent on medication to survive. I know the treatment serves a purpose, but it can never remove the anxiety in the depth of my being that yet another dark cloud is looming, and that I'm back in the hole again. This constant fear is crippling, and I don't want to have to live with it. I have no claim on your power beyond your love, and my own desperation.

Please, please, let me know your love. Let its warmth melt the fog, penetrate the darkness, and dispel the gloom. I feel I have nothing to offer but my cry and my despair. I cannot pretend to have great hope, or any great depth of faith, because when I feel like this I am conscious of nothing but the darkness. Somehow, in the midst of it all, however, I continue to hope against hope, because you are the only one who can get to where I am now. Even my best friends can have no idea what is going on inside me, and I feel powerless to let them enter there. I wouldn't know where to start, and I don't believe it would make much sense, even if I shared with them. There are times when I suspect that I'm going crazy, and, I fear that any attempt to share with them how exactly I'm feeling, would only succeed in confirming that fact to them.

Jesus, Lord, I have often heard it said that you came as a light to the nations, as a light to those who sat in darkness, and in the shadow of death. Please, please come into the dark cave of my soul, of my spirit, and bring your light to dispel the darkness. Please free me from my bondage, from my prison. Visit me in my solitary cell, and enkindle within me the spark of hope and of faith. Surely where you are there can be no darkness. I often think of you crying out on Calvary, as if the Father himself had abandoned you. You know what it's like to feel utterly alone. In Gethsemane, when the apostles kept falling asleep, you experienced the darkness of that hour. Somehow, I believe that you understand, and I feel I can open my heart to you, and let you see me exactly as I am. I don't really know how I am, to be honest with you, because I seem to have lost my inner sensitivity, and even my feelings are unclear, and hard to describe or distinguish. In the darkness, I'm not too clear where the door of my heart and soul are, but I trust you to find that. One of my reactions to this awful experience of depression, and inner darkness, is that I get to a stage where I just don't care any more, one way or another. In my present cry, there is no order or priority, because I just don't know where, or how, you could start to set me free. With my finger nails, I cling to the hope that, in the midst of it all, you can see what I cannot see, you can go where I cannot go, and you certainly can do what I myself could never do.

Lord, I think of all those times in the gospels when you entered the darkness of other people's lives; when you healed the blind, raised the dead, and gave hope to those in desperation. I remember you walking into the life of the widow of Naim, who had lost everything, and you restored her son, and her joy. You reached out your hand to Peter as he sank in the waters, and your raised your hand to quell the raging storm. Lord, I believe, help my unbelief. Lord, increase my faith. Lord, to whom else can I go? I believe that you are the Christ who has come into the world. Even as I speak to you, I can experience a spark of hope being lit within my heart. It was for people like me that you came. You came to find the lost ones, and to bring them safely home. You came to give freedom to captives, and light to those in darkness. Without wishing to be dramatic, Lord, with all my heart I now believe that I qualify as one of those you came to redeem, to set free. My faith cannot stretch far enough to accept that there might be some good purpose in my depression, but if it means that I have a deep personal encounter with you in that darkness, then it surely will have led to a good. There were many people in the gospels who made contact with you in the most unusual and unlikely ways, whether it was up in a sycamore tree, or being lowered through a roof on a stretcher. Nicodemus came to meet you in the dark of night, and you walked with distraught and defeated disciples all the way to Emmaus. Lord, if this is your way of entering my life, then I can accept it. I can accept it, because I believe that if you make your home in my heart, that the darkness will be dispelled, and that the lights will come on again.

Spirit of God, you came to enlighten us, and to guide our feet into the ways of peace. You came to be our Comforter, to complete the work of Jesus, and to bring us the fullness of grace. Grace is gift, total gift, and that is why I dare ask you for the grace of enlightenment, of hope, and of faith. Please flood my soul with light and with life. Roll away the stone from my heart, and let the doors of that room be thrown open once again. Lead me out into the light. Jesus said that you would never leave us, so, with all my heart, I ask you, please never to leave me, and may your presence, and the light of your presence, be the one constant experience in my life. When I am trapped in the midst of a depression, it appears as if you have left me, deserted me, and I return to clay again. As the Hebrews made their way through the desert, for forty years, towards the Promised Land, you accompanied them all the way. In the heat of midday, you were a cloud to protect them from the desert heat, and in the cold of the night, you were a fire to keep them warm. You hovered over the waters, at the time of creation, and brought order out of chaos. I keep reminding myself of this, as I turn to you. I open my hands and my heart, just as I open my lungs with a deep breath, and I invite you to fill the sails of my boat, so I can move on, and not remain stuck in the one spot. Please give me lift-off out of the quicksand of terror, when I experience myself sinking, without hope. Spirit, Breath, and Power of God, please breathe power and life into me now, so that I may live again. Like the dry bones in the vision of the prophet, please bring the bones together, put flesh on them, and breathe life into them, so that I can live and walk in your power. Thank you.

Listen…
My dear dear child, my friend, thank you for turning to me, and for pouring out your heart to me. I am always on 'stand-by', waiting for any of my children to call to me. I didn't create you to be miserable, to be lost, to be a failure. I gave you life, and I want you to live that life to the full. My grace builds on human nature, but it does not, or never will replace it. Therefore, at the end of the day, you are still a human being, who is heir to all the frailties that go with being human. Human nature is very very complex. It is full of emotions, drives, instincts, inclinations, moods, etc, etc. You are created in such a way that, left to your own devices, you can do anything you choose, you can go down any road you select. I know what is best for you, but I cannot deprive you of your choices, of your free-will. There is something that is inbuilt into your nature, which you call conscience. In simple language, that is a way of knowing things. (You notice the word 'science' as part of the word?) In other words, because of your

conscience, you, too, know instinctively what is best for you. It is like some little inner voice that approves or disapproves whenever you do something. Original sin was the result of believing or accepting a lie. All the damage to human nature flowed from that. It follows, then, that the only antidote to that is truth and honesty.

Thank you for being honest about how you feel. The road to truth is the road to health. Depression is often brought about by an inability to share what's happening within. We 'bottle' things up, as it were; we bury our emotions, we don't cry, and we insist that we're not really angry. Eventually the system becomes clogged up with unclaimed and unnamed emotions, and, like the engine of a car with no oil, our insides completely seize up, and we grind to a halt. It may seem simplistic to speak of the lack of a lubricant in the soul, but that really is part of the problem. The soul can become cluttered with repressed emotions, and unexpressed desires, hurts, angers, etc. You become as sick as your secrets. Satan loves the darkness, the secrecy, the festering unexpressed grievance. It is exposed and overcome when you open your heart totally to me, and acknowledge things just as they are. I am not at all in the business of apportioning blame here. It matters little how you got into your present predicament. It matters greatly, however, that you know how to get out of it. Thank you for turning to me at this time.

I am not interested in simply lifting a cloud of depression. I need and want to get underneath the sickness, to eliminate the causes; otherwise, in no time at all, you are back in the cloud again. My Spirit is like a fountain of living water, deep down at the core of your being. You may feel as dry as a desert, but, don't forget that beneath every desert there is plenty of water. I want that water to rise to the surface, so that you become an oasis, which gives abundant life to yourself and to those around you. What is preventing that happening is the amount of wreckage and garbage that has gathered within your spirit. You have to be willing to get rid of all of that, if you want to be free. Like an engine with dirty oil, or a computer with a virus, you have to clear out all of those things that fill you up, and weigh you down. You have to get down to some serious stock-taking, that will enable you to name, claim, and tame your demons. You can do this through counselling, therapy, doing a full moral inventory of yourself, and sharing that with someone you can trust, or, if your religious upbringing has been within the Roman Catholic Church, then you could do nothing better than make a general Confession, where you could unload all that weighs you down and cast it into the sea of my mercy, forgiveness and love.

Jesus told you that I would surely give the Holy Spirit to those who ask. Implied in everything you have said is a clear request to be filled with my Spirit. It means entering into a whole new way of living and of being. If you live by the standards of the world, you find your power and your strength in material things, in wealth, politics, social status, etc. If you want to live in my kingdom, then you have to accept that I will supply the power. That Power is the Spirit. That Spirit has to become for your inner being what your breath is to your body. When you are in a state of depression, you experience a sense of deadness deep within your spirit. The fire has gone out, the light is switched off. It is into that very place that I want to breathe my Spirit, to enkindle within you the fire of divine love. It is right there, at the very core of your being, that you are your most real, your most authentic self. It is there, also, that all of your human weaknesses are to be found. That is why you must think of my Spirit as a burning fire, entering the very core of your being, ready to burn the rubbish, and to melt the ice. It is there that the Spirit wishes to flood you with light from within.

Living in my kingdom is really very simple. It means that Jesus is Lord, and that the Holy Spirit is the power. If my Son Jesus is Lord, then you will allow him take charge of everything, and if my Spirit is to provide the power, then you will do nothing, literally nothing without involving and including my Spirit. 'Whether you eat, or drink, or whatever else you do...' is how the Bible speaks of this. At the beginning of each day you go on your knees, hand the day over, and ask for help. At the end of each day you go on your knees and give thanks. You have to learn to live and to walk in the power of my Spirit. This may not be easy for you because, after years of worry, self-centredness, self-preoccupation, and trying to run the show yourself, you will have developed a pattern of behaviour that may not easily be broken. Old habits die hard. That is why I want you to live in the power of my Spirit. Don't go out the door, make a decision, make a phone call, undertake a task, without first getting in touch with the Spirit that is dwelling within your heart. That Spirit will never leave you, but if you continue to do things your way, then in effect you are on your own. And you cannot make it on your own. Of that you can be certain.

I said earlier that you have to develop a whole new way of being and of living. This is going to involve prayer. By this I don't mean saying prayers. It means being in touch with your heart, where the Divinity dwells. It means going aside for short periods, where you can be still, let the muddy water within your heart settle down, and be conscious of the Presence within. Words are not necessary for this. This is reflection, which is sometimes called meditation, or contemplation. It is taking time out to go downstairs, to be in touch with where the Power lies. You carry that Power around within you, and you are never one moment without that Power being there with you. On a human level, you may be a naturally depressive person, who is pessimistic and worried about everything, always expecting the worst to happen. In your case, no long-term resolutions will work, because you will naturally tend to drift back into your old ways. With you, this present moment is the most precious moment of your whole life. What I mean by that is that you can live in peace for only one moment at a time. At each and every step of the way, you have to practice becoming a person of NOW, where, just for now, you will do exactly as I have told you. I want you to reflect on developing the attitude that continually reminds you that: whatever I am doing, wherever I am going, whoever I'm with, I am walking in the Power of my God within. Nothing, but nothing, can harm me or come between me and that Presence. It is almost as if there was someone else walking in front of you, every moment of every day, making smooth the path ahead, and holding up a placard with the words: Nothing will happen, nothing will go wrong, nothing will change unless you decide, unless you want it to. In a way, in a very real way indeed, I am asking you to go back to school! You have to return to the very basics of living. Surely, living in the NOW is only common-sense, isn't it? You cannot change yesterday, and you have no control over tomorrow, so why not live today, enjoy it, and make the most of it?

I have given you life, and I offer you everything it takes to live that life to the full. Notice I use the word offer, because you must be free to accept or reject. You don't have to accept any of my gifts. I never want you to be depressed, lonely, afraid, or lost. That has never been my will or intention for you. I want you to experience my Presence at all times. One problem you might have with this is that you may be trying to understand it. That is not possible for you, with mere human intellect. All I ask is that you *experience* my presence firstly, and perhaps you might come to understand something about it at a later date. My Spirit rises up from within you. In other words, it doesn't begin in your head! It begins in your heart, at the core of your being, like living water beneath the driest desert, and it rises up within you, to dispel the dryness, to refresh the spirit. Pride is a major obstacle to my work in the human heart. It is the on-going presence of Original Sin, that was a sin of pride in the first place. 'Human' comes from the word 'humus', which means clay. 'Humility' comes from the word 'humilitas', which means of the earth. You are totally subject to the law of gravity, and by yourself, and on your own, you can only go down. That is a simple basic fact of life. Humility does not consist in believing that you are no good, or not as good as others. Humility is truth, and that means accepting the basic truths about yourself and your human condition. It may seem a paradox, but you are at your greatest strength when you are prepared to admit your weaknesses. It is then, and only then, that my Power can be seen at its best, that the Spirit can take over and become your strength.

You turned to me because you were depressed. Thank you for that. In my response I do not promise some sort of stop-gap solution that will get you by for a week or two. I want to fill you with such life and such love that your heart will be filled with gratitude and, with time, you will come to know that it is not possible to be grateful and unhappy at the same time. Mary sàng her Magnificat. She magnified the Lord. The bigger your God, the smaller your problems. The only limits to what I can do in your life are the ones you yourself set. OK? Let's begin again ... you are not alone ... I am walking with you. There is a Power within you that is greater than all the other powers you can meet on the road of life. With me, you will win ... All I ask is that you accept and believe that ...

11. I have cancer, Lord

Speak…

Lord, you know me through and through. You know my every thought. You know my lonely moments, my quiet fears, my greatest guilt. You can read my heart like an open book. Because you can read my thoughts, you know that I have often reflected on life, on death; on when and how I would die, and how all that would be. To a large extent I always tried to keep that at arm's length, because it was too uncomfortable to let too close. Of course, I knew I would die some day, but that had nothing whatever to do with my life just now. And then I heard that dreaded word cancer, the Big C, and the bottom fell out of my life. The immediate shock was the worst, before I had time to discuss it, listen to the doctor, or look at the news objectively. I know there will come a time, some day, when the word 'cancer' will mean no more than 'tonsillitis' or 'appendicitis' means today. In my parents' time, TB or diphtheria sent a shudder throughout the whole community, effecting more than the person who had contracted it. Cancer is a bit closer to our time, however, and, while medical research and treatment has come a long long way, and while the graph of recoveries continues to rise, there is, however, a very real dread of the diagnosis of cancer.

I know I have two clear choices: I can fold up, go to bed and die, or I can turn this into the greatest time in my whole life. If I choose the latter, I can grasp life with a much firmer grip, with a greater sense of appreciation and responsibility for how I live it, and I can become much more alive than I have ever been up till now. Jesus, Lord, you came to redeem, to save, to heal, and to give us life in abundance. I don't think it too far-fetched that having cancer might open me, at last, to all that you offer. Nothing is impossible to you, and you can always turn everything into good, no matter how bad it may seem to us. I don't come crawling to you, because I know you don't want that; that would be an insult to your great love. I turn to you because I choose to, because I am free to, and because you want me to. I turn to you, because you, and you alone, can take my present situation and turn it into a good.

One of my first reactions, when I heard the word cancer, was to experience a sense of helplessness. The only hope I clung to was that the diagnosis was wrong, and that further checks would prove that to be so. My head was in a spin, and the questions were flying Why? Why me? Why now? Why this? I know rightly, Lord, that you understand all of this totally, and that you allow me deal with my own humanity, and all that is stirred up there, before I am ready to turn to you, and to turn things over to you. You are always and ever on standby, with the extraordinary patience and understanding that goes with extraordinary love. Lord, I don't pretend at all to be in control of things at the moment. I'm getting by, sometimes OK, and sometimes very poorly. I try to generate some inner power and strength of my own, and just when I think I'm in control, something happens and the walls close in again. For someone who has always been able to cope, it is difficult for me to have to admit that, this time around, I experience myself as very brittle, very frail, very fragile. It's really hard to keep up appearances, to disguise my worries, and to hide my worst fears. Deep down within me is a very strong desire to go on living. I'm just not prepared to go to bed and wait for death. I believe that strength must come from you, and I am grateful for that.

Only you, Lord, can understand the human mind, and how it works. My mind tells me that I have cancer, not just that I am sick. My mind wishes that it was anything else but what I have. There were many times in my life when I wished

I were anywhere else than where I was. I find it really difficult
to face reality, and to be prepared to live in that reality. I know
that you are real and, until I become real and live in and with
my reality, there is no chance that we can come face to face.
And yes, Lord, that is what I want to do right now. I don't
want to wait till I die before coming face to face with you. You
know me through and through, and so there's no point in trying to pretend, or trying to choose nice words, flowery language, or impressive speeches, when I come before you. I
stand before you now, exactly as I am, with all my fears, worries, anxieties, and doubts, and I pray 'Lord, please help me.
Please place your healing hand upon me. You only have to
say the word, and I will be healed.' I don't understand faith
too well. I always thought that, if I had faith, I would never
have doubts. Now I'm beginning to accept that that cannot be
so, or at least, that is impossible for me. With all my doubts,
with all my worries, with all my fears, above all of that rises
the belief that you can heal me. It is as if my faith in you rises
above all the rest, when I become still within, let the muddy
water settle, and become aware of your presence within me. I
am beginning to see that faith has really very little to do with
how I feel, how I believe, or how good I am. I am also beginning to see that faith can actually be accompanied by doubts
and, it is in spite of the doubts, that my faith grows. I know
that you love me, and it is from that fact, and from that fact
alone, that my faith comes. This has nothing to do with
church, religion, prayers, or practice. On my side, I have
nothing to offer but my fears, my brokenness and, yes, my
cancer. If I concentrated on my side of the equation, I would
be in the depths of despair long ago. In fact it is not an equation, except that you can equate my nothingness with your
everything, my fears with your peace, my sickness with your
health.

As I speak to you, Lord, I'm beginning to get some sense
of the old paint being stripped away within my soul. I have a
sense of being purified, of being stripped naked before you,

of being totally exposed to your love. I have lived so much of my life in smugness and in cozy confidence. I went about my business without a care in the world. I took my health for granted, I took my life for granted. I attended funerals, walked away, and continued to keep life sufficiently on the surface so that nothing really penetrated my outward veneer of coolness and calm. I was in control, and nothing really bad could happen to me. It was always somebody else's funeral. I don't pretend to understand, Lord, but I suspect that I may well need this cancer, to help concentrate my thinking, and deepen my living. I believe that you are more interested in the depth of my life than in the length of it. You are more interested in quality than in quantity. While I worry about the next life, you are concerned that there may not be much life going on now. In your eyes I'm not dying but, in your eyes I may not be living either. I believe it is your wish that I should live life fully, and live it right out to the end. I don't believe that you ever pluck a flower from the garden of life until you decide that the time is right.

Lord, my own understanding of incarnation is that you came down here on earth to meet us and to be with us as we are. You easily could have loved us from a distance, but you decided not to. Incarnation, for me, at this moment, is that you want to come to me as I am, right here, right now. Reality for me is that, yes, I do have cancer, but that does not mean that it is terminal. My life is terminal, I know, but because of you, I can have much of life to live still. Please help me accept the reality of my situation, to accept things as they are. Out of that reality will come a prayer that is from the heart, a prayer that wells up from within the depths of my soul, a prayer that will always reach and touch your heart. In the past much of my praying could have been nothing more than words, coming from my lips, but not from my heart. I now feel that it is not possible for a human being to fall on her knees, cry out to you, and not be heard. Lord, Jesus, Son of David, Son of God, hear me, heal me, save me.

Listen...

Thank you, my child, my friend, for that prayer from the heart. My grace works wonders in a heart like yours. Please accept that I know what I'm doing, and that you, and your welfare, are at the very core of all my plans for you. I would never let anything happen to you that would harm you, unless you yourself opted for that yourself. In that case, I could do nothing because of my respect for your free-will. As you said, I know you through and through, and I understand only too well that it often takes something like cancer to turn the human mind totally to me. Please believe me when I say that that is not why I permit cancer to occur. In actual fact, believe it or not, it is not I that gave you cancer. You inherited it, your personality incubated it, or your life-style has caused it. How you got cancer is totally unimportant at the moment. The point is that you have it, and that you want me to remove it, arrest it, or contain it. I understand only too well why you should turn to me with all your heart, at this time, more than before. It is very natural and very human to do this. As I said in the gospel, 'It is not the healthy who need the physician, but the sick'. I don't expect you to come running to me in panic every moment of every day, no more than I would want you to be running to your doctor, your dentist, or your physio every single day. You know they are there if and when you want them. You know that I am here, that you have to travel no further than your heart to find me, and that you don't need words when you stand before me. It pleases me greatly when you are aware of my presence, because this can help you through the lonely moments, the sleepless nights, or the troubled days. I am in your heart for your sake, and for your sake only. That is why I came on earth in the first place. My healing must begin within your heart. My life must flow through your veins, my Spirit must radiate your body, if you want me to remove all growths that are not part of the person my Father created. I came that you should have life, and I don't want anything to destroy or limit your living of that life.

I can use anything and everything for good. Even your sins of the past can generate great compassion within you today. I have no desire to waste anything, and I can turn everything into good. At the moment you think of yourself as having cancer, and that is the extent of your knowledge of how you are. You cannot possibly see other areas of your life where healing is more urgently needed. I can see many many areas within you that are in need of healing. I am not interested in healing just one area, and allowing you remain unhealthy. 'Your sins are forgiven, arise and walk', was my way of showing that healing begins on the inside and works out from there. You couldn't imagine me healing a blind man, and letting him go down the road full of resentment towards his brother. In that case, the man wasn't healed, but continued to be very very blind indeed. What I'm asking you is to put the whole lot on the line. When I washed the apostles' feet, I said 'You are clean, but not all'. In your case I want all of you to be healed, and the fact that you have cancer provides a good opportunity for you to open out your whole being to me, and for me to touch everything within you that is in need of healing. This is a moment of grace, it is an opportunity of great blessing, an occasion for great growth. If you think of cancer being a growth, or as something that should not be there, then please let me include with that everything else within you that should not be there either. I want you totally healed; otherwise you are not healed at all.

It may surprise you to know some of the more serious barriers to my Power working within you. It has little to do with religion, practice, prayers, or anything like that. The biggest barriers are anger, resentments, and unforgiveness. In themselves, these are destructive, and my power cannot work alongside these. Having a resentment against another is like you are drinking poison, and you are expecting the other person to die. I know it sounds crazy, but it is very seriously crazy. A soul that is filled with unforgiveness is certainly not in a healing mode; healing cannot take place there. This is something very serious, and I want you to give it your full attention. Of course, I want to heal you, but you must provide the conditions for healing to take place. I certainly will help you, I will give you what you need, but you must be willing to let go, to rid your heart, and to prepare your spirit. I know rightly that others have hurt you. I know only too well where the resentments are coming from, and I am very aware of the source of the anger. That makes no difference, however. They have to go if you are to be healed. It is never a question of will-power. You don't have what it takes to deal with all of this on your own. If you have the will, I will supply the power. Like the man at the pool, in the gospels, I am now asking you : 'Do you want to be healed?' Oh yes, of course, you want to get rid of your cancer, you want that to be taken away. However, my child, my friend, you will still not be healed, you will still be quite sick. That is not my wish for you.

Speaking of forgiveness, how about beginning with forgiving yourself? That may surprise you, but if you dig a little into your thoughts and memories, you will find plenty of guilt, regrets, hindsights, and misgivings. Part of you blames yourself for the cancer. You contributed to it through some pattern of behaviour, through your use or abuse of food, nicotine, alcohol; through fretting, worrying, or anxiety; or indeed though the accumulation of the emotional or spiritual toxins of unforgiveness, angers and resentments. As your God, I ask you to open out the canvas of your life to me ... out ... out ... right out to the very corners. Nothing hidden, nothing denied; the good, the bad, and the ugly. Now, let us look at this together. Do you see what I see? Do you want to see what I see? Are you prepared to face and accept the reality of what you see? There is nothing really serious there. That's not what I have in mind. I'm not here to accuse you or condemn you. I am here to heal you. All I need is that you honestly admit and accept all the guilt, the regrets, the failures, the sins, and the brokenness that this canvas of your life is reflecting back to you.

(Take a few moments out now, to reflect on the canvas of your life, so that you can sincerely acknowledge and accept the reality of what it reflects.)

I now want to erase those from the canvas, to tell you that they are forgiven, and to ask you to join me in total forgiveness of yourself. OK, so far? There is a difference between being healed and being cured. To be healed means to be restored to health, and to be cured is to have some illness removed. I have much more interested in the ministry of healing, because I want all of you to be healthy. In the gospels I speak of my joy, my peace, and my abundant life. I want nothing less for you. I'm sure you are quite aware how human organisations like the UN, NATO, etc, may succeed in stopping a war, but they cannot bring peace. The war breaks out again, further down the road, or in some other country. What I am offering is not just some quick-fix that will allay your immediate fears. I am thinking of a whole new way of living, of being, and of recovering. I am now inviting you into a programme of recovery which, like the incoming tide, will lift all the boats, even those stuck in the mud. I want to raise you up, I want you to experience a whole new way of living, of thinking, and of seeing things. One of the effects of getting something like cancer is to concentrate the focus of one's attention on the next life; whereas I continue to try to turn the focus of your attention onto this life. This is the life you should be concerned about; the quality, the depth, the investment, and the incarnational dimension. Heaven begins now, and you have to begin to find that heaven, that kingdom within your own heart. Seek that kingdom first, and everything else will be added to you. Leave the cancer to me; you have enough to be getting on with. The very fact that you have cancer may be exactly what you need to open up your heart, your mind, and your spirit to a much wider and fuller living and experience of living. Life becomes precious when each day is cherished. You can get so involved with the urgent that you overlook the important. I never waste anything, whether it be experience, failure, sickness, or sin. I can turn everything into good, if it is given to me. What you see as a problem, I can see as an opportunity. I can see the beauty of the tapestry, whereas from where you are, you can see only the reverse side, with threads going in all directions, with no apparent pattern, design or order.

It is not my wish, my intention, or my will that you should not be concerned, anxious, worried, or afraid, because you have cancer. You are a human being, and your reaction is the normal reaction of any normal human being. All I am asking is that you may be willing to let me into the situation, in such a way that you do not have to continue as if I were indifferent, unaware, or unwilling to become involved. All I have ever looked for from anyone is that I be believed, that I be accepted, that I be allowed do what I came to do. Healing the sick, replacing that sickness with abundant life, replacing the fear with my peace, and restoring the hope in the heart of the anxious one ... that, in brief, is central to my mission and presence among you. Someone said one time that if I had to break your heart, and break every bone in your body, I would do so if that resulted in you letting me take over the running of your day-to-day living. That, of course, is not true, because the statement is made the wrong way around. I was the one who was willing to have my heart and every bone of my body broken, so that I could become Lord in your heart, and God in your life. I love you, and I see your present situation affording me a very special opportunity to let you experience my love. You are mine. You did not choose me. No, I have chosen you, and instead of you making promises, or any great commitment to me now, all I ask is that your accept and believe the very clear and the very definite promises I have made to you. Heaven and earth will pass away before my word passes away.

12. A cry from the bereaved heart

(The person who has died could be anywhere within the range of the still-born or the cot death to an aged grandmother, a spouse, a child, a friend. The death could have been unexpected, as with heart attack, accident, suicide, or murder. It could have involved several loved ones, through fire, car accident, etc. Because of all these possibilities, I will not attempt to write a prayer that would cover all eventualities. Rather will I make a few suggestions that might 'kick-start' your own personal prayer, and leave you alone with your God. My main attempt, in this chapter, will be to share what I believe the good Lord might want to say to you now, in the midst of all your pain.)

Dear Lord, I'm really hurting. I know that death is a fact of life. I see lists of death notices in every newspaper I read. For so long, death seemed to me something that happened to some family somewhere else. But this time, Lord, it has hit me, and I'm caught up in the pain, in the reality...

Death never seems to come at the right time. For some, it comes too soon, and for others it seems to be long overdue ... In my case ...

I know that once a baby is born it is born to die. That is the only fact of life that we already know about this newborn infant ...

Death frightens me, and puzzles me, because I just don't understand it. The timing and the circumstances are so unpredictable as to appear haphazard and at random. There seems to be no order of selection, where children bury their parents, or whether people are good, bad, productive, or destructive ...

No matter what the Christian faith may teach us, I still experience some sense of finality about the parting. I still expect to meet up again with those who have gone on ahead, but in a very real way, for me at least, life will never be the same again …

I often heard it said that each person is unique, and that no two people are alike. I now know that the loss of a person is unique, and the pain of that loss is also unique. The pain I now feel is my own personal pain at the loss of that particular person …

I had often heard it said that guilt can be part of the grieving process, and that had puzzled me. Now I know what is meant by that. All the things I didn't do, all the things I didn't say … now it's too late. There are also the things that I did say and do that I regret …

For so much of my life I tended to just plod along, taking things for granted, and not wishing to reflect too deeply on the realities or the possibilities. Now I am stopped in my tracks, as I waken up to the reality of what has happened …

I know that this time gives me an opportunity to really examine my beliefs, my faith, and my convictions. I'm not looking for some sort of 'holy balm' to cover over the hurt and make it go away. I know rightly that I must go through the pain, if I am to come through this with greater strength. I'm not looking for any 'quick-fix' that will make everything different, and insulate me from the reality of what has happened, or how I feel. I just ask you, Lord, to help me through this time, and to enable me find you in some new way. Somewhere within me is the hope that, by doing so, I will strengthen the bond with the one I have lost, and that I can come to a deeper conviction, and a deeper awareness of what life and death is all about.

Listen…
My dear child, thank you for turning to me in the midst of your pain. I understand how you feel, and I can even under-

stand if you have experienced anger at what you consider I have allowed happen to you. I, too, know what it feels like to cry at a graveside. When I lived on this earth, just like you, I too lost a very close friend in Lazarus. When I met the widow of Naim, following the dead body of her only son, I was deeply moved, and I relieved her pain. (Don't forget that Lazarus and the widow's son still had to die at a later date, so things were postponed rather than solved.) All of this happened before I myself passed through the gates of death. In doing so, I overcame death, and it was of primary importance to me to convince the apostles, beyond all shadow of doubt, that I had overcome death, and it was no longer an enemy. In the story of creation, after God created anything, like the planets, the waters, the earth, etc, the Bible says, 'And he saw that it was good'. Sin, sickness, and death were not part of that creation. These are like the weeds among the good wheat in the gospel story. They are the direct results of original sin. It was to remove all three that I came.

When I publicly joined the sinners that came to John the Baptist at the Jordan river, I took upon my own shoulders the sins of the whole world. My Calvary began from that moment. It was then that 'the heavens were opened', the Holy Spirit was seen to come upon me, and the Father's voice was heard, calling on the people to listen to me. When I bowed my head in death 'the veil of the Holy of Holies in the Temple was torn in two'. The heavens were opened once again, and it was now possible for you, and all of yours, to enter the Holy of Holies, to come right into the presence of God. That was made possible by my death. I paid the price so that you and yours could enter heaven, could return to the Garden.

Life is a journey, and once it begins, it never ends. There are three stages in that journey. There is the womb-life, the womb of life, and the fullness of life. Under normal circumstances, the womb-life is a fairly fixed and definite time. The fullness of life is eternal, never ending. It is the womb of life itself that presents the problems. Death itself is certain; it is life that is uncertain. As I said, life is a journey, but it is a journey that you have never travelled before. In other words, you don't know what's to be seen around the next corner. It is a mystery to be lived, rather than a problem to be solved. It is a process of growth, a journey of discovery. Each person continues to be part of my creation, within my love and care, and destined for eternal life with me. The problem with life is that there are many many factors in life which I do not predestine or predict, because of the free-will of each individual, and the inherent frailties of human life itself. The body is like a very delicate earthen vessel, subject to all the pressures, hardships, violence, diseases, and mishaps of human living. The body is not you. You are a spiritual being, living in a frail human body for a relatively short while, and at any time, for whatever reason, the body can break down, can fold up, and can cease to function. It is then time to leave the body, and go ahead to the third and final stage of life, when you join me in a whole new life that is eternal, free from all the hardships of human living. The timing of this is subject to a combination of millions of factors, most of them of human origin, and the effects of human situations, circumstances, and events.

I know it is very difficult for you to understand all of this. It may seem, at times, as if I just don't care, or I don't want to get involved. My love for you, my plan for your eternal happiness, and my accompanying you on your journey, never ever ceases to be. If I were to protect you from all the hardships of life, and to smooth out every step of your journey, then I am depriving you of growth, and interfering in your choices, and greatly limiting your options. I never wanted Judas to go out and hang himself, but I couldn't stop him if he chose to do so. My love and my presence is totally and completely with you, no matter what happens to you. If I am with you only when things are going well for you, then I could not claim to really love you at all. It can be very hard to appreciate how I can be with someone, and yet allow nature take its course in the life of that person. For example, someone gets

cancer. It was not I that gave that cancer, or that I decided that
this person should have cancer. Nature, inheritance, food,
patterns of behaviour, etc has brought about the cancer. My
grace builds on nature, it doesn't replace it. In other words, I
will not manipulate you, nor will I attempt to manipulate
human nature, everyday events, or the passing of time. I am
there with you, I am there for you, and I will always be there
within you. What I mean is that nothing will ever happen to
you that yourself and myself together will not be able to handle.

I am very conscious now that, in the midst of all your
hurts, you certainly don't need some intellectual discussion.
You are experiencing the pain of loss, and that is very real,
and no amount of reasoning up in the head is going to ease
that pain. Life is a whole series of letting-goes. The cord is cut
at birth, and this can be followed by post-natal depression,
where the system is reacting to a loss. Bereavement is like an
amputation, where a limb has been removed. It will be possible to walk again, but certainly not for a while. Time is the
great healer for the bereaved. This does not imply forgetting,
but continuing to remember. 'Do this in memory of me' can
spur many a new enterprise for the benefit of others. Quite a
lot of the groups that help those experiencing bereavement of
one kind or another, are made up of people who themselves
experienced bereavement, and who felt totally alone in the
pain, and had nowhere to turn.

Quite often you may hear the phrase that 'Sure it's the will
of God'. That is not always true. It is not my will that children
die of hunger, that the unborn are denied their right to life, or
that someone is brutally murdered. It is not my will that a
young mother should live with great expectations, only to be
faced with a still-birth, or a cot death. It is not my will that
someone should be so overcome by life that he should choose
to end it, or that some innocent passer-by should get caught
in the force of an explosion. I have never planted a bomb or
fired a bullet. I have never arranged things so that half the

world should be dying of hunger, while the other half is on a diet, trying to lose weight. It was to prevent all this that I came on earth. From that first Christmas night, there continue to be doors and hearts closed to me and to my message. I cry out for witnesses to my message, and for others to heed the witnesses. Because people did not like the message, they have often shot the messenger. But the message is still the same. There is a spiritual arms-race on for the souls and hearts of people. All I can guarantee is that evil will never succeed, but I need witnesses to show that goodness can triumph over evil.

It is obvious that you have lost someone you dearly loved. Please accept the fact that I love that person also, and that my love will continue to safeguard, to hold, and to keep that person from all harm. You wouldn't want that person to be anything but completely happy after death. You would want the fullness of life and happiness, and eternal freedom from hurt or pain, for the one you have lost. I don't mean this as a put-down, but the best way you can continue to express your love is to entrust your beloved one to me, and to my Father's eternal hug. Those who have died have not gone away; they have simply gone ahead. It is certainly and literally a case of *au revoir*, and not goodbye. Until you meet again ... Faith is a response to my love, even when you cannot understand it. Sometimes you can manage nothing more than blind faith, where you just hang in there, and cling to the hope that all will be well. Loss of hope is the one great disaster for the Christian. The falling leaves of autumn is not a cause of despair, even if it is followed by a harsh bleak winter. You know that spring will come, and all those seeds, now dormant in the ground, will come to life, and all of nature will be born again. In the Bible are the words, 'There is a time for everything, a season for every activity under heaven.' This earth is not your home; you are just passing through. You are part of a pilgrim people, on your way home to the Promised Land. Death is like the Red Sea, through which all must pass to enter that land. In the Old Testament, Moses was the leader. Now it's I myself who leads you. If you follow me you will not walk in darkness, but will have the light of life. There will, of course, be dark moments, because life consists of ups and downs and, until you reach total freedom in death, struggle will always be part of human living. It is in the times of struggle that real growth occurs, and it is in the moment of darkness that you often turn to me with a more open heart.

I want you to listen to the words of the gospels again. They were not spoken as a once-off for a particular person at a particular time. The gospel is now, and you are part of it. In some way or other, you are every person in the gospel, and the words are spoken now. Despite your hurt, despite your possible anger, confusion, and loneliness, the very fact that you have listened to me thus far is an indication that you might be ready to hear more. Try to hear these words with your heart, so that my Spirit can enter your heart through the words that you hear. 'I have come that you may have life, and have it to the full ... I will never abandon you, or leave you alone in the storm ... It is not the will of your heavenly Father that any of those entrusted to me should be lost ... Like a woman in labour, you have struggle now ... you have sorrow now, but your sorrow will be turned into joy ... In my Father's house there are many mansions ... I am going to pre-pare a place for you ... and when I have prepared a place for you, I will come and bring you, so that, where I am, you also will be ... You are sad now because I must leave you, but your joy will be great when you see me again ... and your joy no one will take from you ... The sin of this world is unbelief in me ... Woman, why do you weep? ... Why do you doubt? ... I have overcome death ... I have put all your enemies under my feet ... Your names are registered as citizens of heaven ... There is so much more that I want to tell you, but you can't bear it now ... but my Spirit of truth will guide you into all truth, and the truth will set you free; and, if the Spirit sets you free, you will be free indeed.'

Please notice that I have not asked you not to grieve, not to feel the real sense of loss that is yours. Grief is the price you pay for love, and if you never want to cry at a funeral, then don't ever love anyone. That thought is repugnant both to you and to me. There is a direct connection between post-natal depression and bereavement, when the cord is cut or the straps are pulled up out of the grave. The beloved one, who has now gone ahead into the fullness of life, is now all that was intended at the moment of creation, is now all that that person was intended to be. The body is discarded like the booster rockets of a space shuttle, and can fall back to earth, having completed its purpose. The actual person you knew and loved did not go into a coffin, and the 'remains' were but the empty shell of a rocket that has been launched. Death is not the end. As you look out to sea, you cannot see beyond the horizon, even though you know there is so much more beyond your vision. As you look at the sea, your vision is limited to the surface of the water, even though you are well aware that there are millions of gallons beneath your scope of vision. Faith means living without the proof, but certain that the proof will follow. Faith and certainty cannot co-exist, because if there is certainty there is no need for faith. It is normal to have a struggle with the whole area of death, whether that be the loss of a loved one, or the inevitability of your own death. Instead of getting too concerned about life after death, I would be really pleased if you switched your concentration to the quality of your life before death. I am more interested in the depth of your life, rather than the length of it. Everybody dies, but not everybody lives. Perhaps, as you work through your present grief process, you will come out the other end with a greater commitment to what is left of your own life. In doing this, your whole life could be totally transformed, because I would have greater freedom to touch others through you, and your beloved one would certainly be there to inspire and encourage you, as you move forward towards the Great Reunion, when you will never have to say goodbye again.

13. I am worthless, Lord

Speak...

Lord, when I say that I am worthless, I know I don't have to explain to you what exactly I mean by that. I feel, however, in pouring out my heart to you, and in trying to put words on how I feel, that that in itself might be a help. I'm not honestly sure where all this started but, from a very early age, I felt that I wasn't worth much, that I wasn't as good as others, that I just didn't have what many of the others seemed to have. This was confirmed from a very early age through many experiences, many of which were quite painful. This ranged from comparing my family to other families that seemed much better off than we were; from children who had things that my parents couldn't afford; from comparing myself to others in school, to those who were brighter than me, much better in school, at games, school activities, or in general popularity. I always felt that I had to work much harder to get others' attention, or to get their approval. I longed for affirmation, and for assurance that I wasn't exactly an ugly duckling. I would freeze within at the slightest criticism, and I was often deeply hurt by sarcasm, or remarks that confirmed my suspicions that I was, in fact, worthless, and that there was nothing in me that drew admiration or praise from others. I spent much of my time wishing I was someone else. I wished I could sing like that person, play sport like someone else, or had the good looks and charm of another.

I know, as I say this, that there is a great deal of pride inset in all of this. I can see that with hindsight, but my feelings were no less real. I always considered myself as being shy, and I never thought of that as being fear. I was unhappy with how I was or what I had, and I never saw that as ingratitude. I coveted what others had, and I never saw that as jealousy. That's just the way it was, and that was how I felt. I lacked self-confidence, and I was afraid to venture an opinion in case I might sound stupid, or someone might laugh at my ideas. I often fawned, and sought approval, and would do anything to gain that approval. I became a people-pleaser, and I was afraid to say 'no' in case the other person mightn't like me. I carried a great deal of that into life with me. In fact, there is quite a deal of that still within me. Sharing with you openly how I feel gives me hope, because it may well be a step in the right direction. I don't ever want to be aggressive, but I would like to be assertive, to speak my mind, to express my opinion, and not to go on apologising for my existence. I see this as a very real form of bondage that greatly limits the quality of my life.

I know it sounds selfish and ungrateful, Lord, but I thought that you had not given me a fair shake when you created me! In a world of hungry people today, I know that this was pure selfishness and self-centredness. I often wondered why some people seem to be born with a silver spoon in their mouths, while others seem to have nothing going for them. Some people are just naturally gifted in so many ways, while others are just so dull and ordinary. 'Ordinary' might be a good word to describe how I have seen myself for most of my life. In fact I had settled for the ordinary, and just wanted to be good at the ordinary! Oh, of course, I did discover some talent, and I knew I wasn't totally stupid, but the range of my abilities were so limited that I was fearful of stepping outside those perceived limits. I kept myself to myself a great deal, because I was afraid to tell people how I really felt about anything. I tended to agree with others, even when I had opinions that were different. I was conscious of some sort of moral cowardice, but I was too inhibited to take a stand on issues. I felt safer to hide in the crowd, to go with the flow, and to keep my opinions to myself. There were times when all this seemed to gather like a leaden weight within me, and I found it difficult to have any initiative, or to take risks. I now see this as some form of depression, even though I didn't recognise this for what it was at the time.

I always had a great fear of being honest. I hid behind a facade of confidence, even when I was totally unsure of myself within. I was afraid that others might get to really know me, and that they would laugh. I knew that their laugh would kill me, so I played games of pretence, I feigned indifference, and I was willing to be whatever I thought someone perceived me to be. Because of my own discomfit with myself, I was often very uncomfortable in the company of others. My life became a charade, and I could see no escape from my predicament. I harboured resentments, was easily hurt, and I must confess that I sometimes had a good feeling when someone else was seen to fail. I had a serious problem with authority, and I would do anything to achieve or retain their approval. I would complain to others about those in authority, but I would never question or challenge the directions I was given. I was always on my guard in the presence of an authority figure, and I always aimed to please at all costs.

As I recall my experience of growing up, I was very prone to guilt because, Lord, you too were someone in authority, to be served and to be feared. I never actually had any conviction that you loved me. In fact, I felt that you couldn't possibly love me. I suppose I was trying to self-compensate for what others didn't give me, so I tended to be sneaky, underhanded, and dishonest. If others wouldn't give it to me, then, if the opportunity arose, I took it myself. I wanted to be able to have pocket money like everyone else, or to have something to show others that would get their attention. I never understood that love and respect were not items that could be bought. I never understood that, because of my low self-esteem, and lack of appreciation of myself, that I blocked off the possibility of being able to accept the love and respect of others. This low self-esteem meant that I was always giving other people power over me. It was as if I marched to the beat of someone else's drum. I became, on the outside, a total conformist while, within and well disguised, there was a rebel anxious to break out. My anger was often expressed by becoming silent, and I often did not recognise this as anger. I was intimidated by violence, and I would go to any lengths to keep the peace. I was a pacifist through cowardice, and not by any great conviction about the merit of non-violence.

Forgiveness has always been a problem in my life, Lord. I was never good at forgiving myself and, therefore, very slow to forgive others. Oh, I would pretend that all was well but, underneath, I was planning some way to get even, or to ensure that the other person saw the wrong-doing, and would apologise, and thus give me the satisfaction of being proven right. It was very important for me to vindicate myself and, even if I was unable to confront, I looked for other ways to set the record straight. I have never been good at confrontation, because of my lack of confidence and my low self-image. I know of people who became alcoholics because alcohol gave them the buzz, the confidence, and the honesty that they lacked in reality. I can fully understand how this could happen and, providing the alcohol itself didn't take over, I could see great merit in finding new courage in a bottle.

Lord, I am sharing all this with you, because I want to begin to reclaim my life. I want to rid my heart of all the pettiness, the guilt, the self-condemnation, and the feeling of unworthiness. I want to open my heart to your message, and to the hope of the gospel. I ask you, please, to heal every scar of mind and of memory. I ask for a whole new outpouring of your Spirit by way of a Confirmation, that will confirm, empower, and anoint me. My past can explain how I am, but I cannot go on using it as an excuse for how I am. I didn't have control over the past, but I want you to have control over my life from now on. I have no reason whatsoever to trust myself, and I don't want, nor do I ask that I myself might control anything. I know that it is never too late for you. I also know that I have to magnify you, in the sense that my concept of you has been far too small. If you were seen and accepted as all-powerful in my life, then surely a miracle begins right there. It is not a question of self-confidence, but it is about having confidence in you. If you are for me, then who can be against me? If the Father gave you to me, then surely I can trust that he will give me everything else. Lord, I feel it is time to roll back the stone from the tomb of my heart. I have been asleep, or in some sort of non-life for long enough. I know that you are now offering me a whole new chance to begin again, to be born again. Thank you, thank you, Lord, for the grace of salvation, for the grace to start again. I am willing to accept that gift right now, with a grateful and open heart. In my heart I feel that if I change, then my whole life will change. All I can do now is offer you every longing within my heart, every hunger within my soul, every hurt within my memory, and every hope for a whole new future.

Listen…
My dear, dear child, thank you, thank you for pouring your heart out to me. Thank you for the trust and the goodwill. I know you through and through, and I understand you much much better than you could ever understand yourself. You have no idea how much I have longed for this day. I stand at the door and knock, but I cannot enter until you open the door. You are very precious in my sight, and I would like to share with you just exactly what I mean by that. If you can get this one central point, then I know you will become important in your own eyes as well.

In the gospels I told the apostles 'You did not choose me; no, I have chosen you'. You, my friend, did not choose to be born. You had no say whatever in becoming a member of the human race, and in living out your life as a human being. This may be difficult to understand, but let me use several examples to help you see things from my perspective. If you were a teacher, going in to teach a class, it could be expected that you know what you were going to teach today, and what the pupils may know at the end of the class that they may not know now. If you were a builder, building a house, it could be expected that you would have an architect's drawing of the building, right down to the last measurement. In other words, before you begin something, you have some definite idea of what the finished product will be like. When you were created it wasn't just that the Father had nothing better to do! And, by the way, 'God don't make no junk', as one writer put it. At the moment of your creation, you had infinite possibilities, and a life without end. Each person is unique. I'm sure you yourself wouldn't like it if people were clones of each other. Each person is uniquely gifted, and no two people are the same. That is evident if you compare the finger prints of each, or do a DNA blood-test of each. It is as if my Father broke up the mould and threw it away, the moment he created you. Because of hereditary factors, the body of each is obviously different, either in colour, size, or appearance. Personality is like a bag that contains all of one's habits, good and bad. This is the result of both nature and nurture. Part of being human is that you are powerless, of yourself and on your own, your life is unmanageable. It often takes years for people to discover this simple basic truth. Oh, I said this in the gospels in many ways, on many different occasions, but who heard, and who believes me? I said that apart from me you can do nothing, and that I had come in person to lead you on the journey of life into the Promised Land. If it were possible for you to do that on your own, then I need not have taken on your humanity, and travelled the road with you. I'm sure you've often heard the quote, 'For God so loved the world that he sent his only begotten Son, so that those who believe in him may have eternal life.' That word comes alive for you only when you can re-phrase it with conviction 'For God loved me so much ...'

I'm not condemning or blaming you, but a great deal of

your poor self-image, lack of confidence, or self-loathing resulted from the solitary confinement of choosing to be alone
in your world. You yourself were the focus of attention, and
you narrowed your world down to yourself and what concerned you. In simple words, communication is two-way or
no way. You receive back what you yourself give away. If you
don't give, you don't receive. Oh, yes, you gave, but it was
seldom given freely. There was always a price-tag on everything. You gave to gain attention, you performed to merit approval, you existed to meet your own needs through the
crumbs that fell from the tables of others. That was never my
Father's intention for you, when he created you. He has no
favourites, nor has he any grandchildren. You are a child of
God on this earth, with as much right as any other human
being that ever existed. That is central to my teaching on
kingdom living. In the kingdom of the world, people are cat-
egorised all the time, either through ethnic groups, rich, poor,
powerful or disposable. In my kingdom the most disabled
child on this earth has as much right to be here as has the
greatest genius that ever lived.

Beauty is in the eye of the beholder, it is said; but, for me,
beauty is found within the human heart. All the bodies, the
beautiful, the athletic, the disabled, and the plain, will return
to the dust from which they came. When I look within your
heart I see the hurts, the struggles, and the origins of your
present prayer. I want to take you in my arms, to hug you, to
confirm you as someone who is most precious in my eyes. If
you were the only person on this earth, I would still have
come to be with you because, on your own, you could never
make it back to the Garden. At the time of creation there is
frequent use of the phrase 'And God saw that it was good ...'
OK, you have failed, you have sinned, but not because you
are evil, but because you are weak. I love you exactly as you
are, right here, right now. And I love you so much more than
that, and so I don't want you to remain as you are. I want to
redeem you from the slavery of self-hatred, of self-condem-

nation, of self-depreciation. I want to lift you up, to fill your heart with hope, to roll away the stone, to throw open the doors of the upper room and, like Lazarus, to call you to come forth into new life.

You can never find security outside of yourself. The pearl of great price, that for which you search, is hidden within your own heart. No matter what the limits of the body may be, all of God's creatures have within them the capacity to lead a full and worthwhile life. Life is not measured by achievements or accomplishments. There are no brownie points, nor is it marked out of ten. Life is about goodwill, and there is peace on earth to those of goodwill. The only limits of my power working in you and through you are the ones you set. I have endless dreams for you, unbounded possibilities, and nothing less than a call to share in Divinity. I don't waste anything, so I am hoping that you will use all of your sense of worthlessness, all of your moral cowardice, and all of your lack of self-confidence as an incentive to get out of the way, and let me take over the running of your life. Because I am totally present to you now, and you have my full and total attention now, all I ask is that you slow life down to just one day at a time. Just for today, I will lead you every step of the way. Just for today I will not lead you where I won't be there to see you through. Just for today nothing will happen that you and I together will not be able to handle. OK? You might wish to pause here for a few moments to reflect on the simplicity and the seriousness of what it is I am asking from you …

Life is a journey that is made up of many different journeys. In the course of a lifetime several different selves emerge. In other words, you are not the same person you were twenty or thirty years ago. Today is a totally different day from yesterday, and you cannot live today on a Yes of yesterday. There are significant conversion points in the course of a lifetime, when someone opts to turn around, to travel down another road, to decide to take a whole new direction in life. Life is a whole process of being born, of becoming, of gestation. You are now at a whole new and very significant point in your own journey. Thank you for turning to me at this juncture. Thank you for recognising my presence, and my part in the process. Let us move on together from here. In the gospels I identified very strongly with the outcast, the marginalised, and those whom the world ignores. There is some of all of that within you, and that is why I am so pleased that you respond to my invitation, and that you are willing to accept me in a personal way, for specific reasons, and not in some sort of general and superficial acceptance.

There are many many others out there who are now experiencing what you have come through over the years. They desperately need someone to confirm and affirm them. Who better to do that than someone who has been down that same road? Compassion is not something you learn from a book. It is something you can learn and garner from your own hurts, pains, and struggles. Just as I entered into your life to share the burden, the journey, and the struggle with you, so you too can enter into their lives, and become a life-giving person for them. This world is greatly in need of people with hearts full of compassion. They can be my touch-persons in the lives of others. You can turn what was a problem into a wonderful opportunity, what was failure into success, what you saw as worthlessness into eternal riches. Many are called, but few choose to follow. Thank you for laying out your life before me, and for listening to my words of assurance and re-creation. Your life begins right now. Today is the beginning of the rest of your life ...

14. Throughout the day…

Morning…
(Pause for a few moments where a word is followed by '…'. The
slower you go, the more time you give, the more effective this morn-
ing blessing will be.)

This morning I would like to begin by praying for others …
I would like to begin my day by not beginning with myself.
But how can I impart to others the gift of peace and love,
if my own heart is still unloving,
and my own needs are the most important ones,
if this day is something for me, and for me alone,
and I have no peace of mind myself?

So I will begin with my own heart …
I will begin by opening my heart to the Lord …
I bring to the Lord every feeling within,
every feeling of resentment, anger, bitterness,
every feeling of jealousy, unforgiveness, and selfishness
that may still be lurking there;
asking that his grace
will make my heart yield to love some day,
if not right now…

Then I ask for peace …
I list the things that disturb my peace of mind…
and imagine that I place them in God's hands,
I imagine him taking them in his loving care,
in the hope that this will bring me freedom from anxiety,
at least during this time of prayer.

Then I seek the depth that silence brings,
because prayer that springs from silence
is powerful and effective …
I let the muddy water settle within …
I take time out to let a sense of inner calmness
settle within my heart …
So I listen to the sounds around me …
I become aware of the exact circumstances in which I am …
I become aware of the feelings and sensations in my body,
my breathing in and out ...
my heart pumping and the blood flowing,
keeping the fire of life alive within me …

Now I pray for family, friends, and those I love …
I pray for those who asked for my prayers …
Over each of them I say a blessing:
'May you be greatly blessed this day, and may you
be free from all harm and from all evil',
imagining that my prayers, words, and wishes will create
a protective shield of grace around them.

Then I turn to people I dislike,
and people who dislike me …
Over each of them I say this prayer:
'May you and I be friends some day,
may time remove what keeps us from trusting each other,
from loving each other,
and from respecting each other's right to be',
imagining some future scene
when this may come to pass …

I think of anxious people I know …
People whose lives are filled with fear …
People who are depressed …
To each of them I say:
'May you come to know the peace of Christ;

may you come to experience his presence within you,
may you know for certain that you are not alone'
imagining that my prayer for them
will surely be fulfilled.

I think of people who are disabled ...
People who depend on others for their basic cares and
needs...
People whose lives are limited within the confines
of four walls ...
and to each of them I say:
'May you find courage and strength,
may your heart take wings,
and may your zest for life bring you all over the world',
imagining that my prayer unleashes within each of them
resources of which they were totally unaware.

I think of lonely people ...
People lacking love, or a sense of belonging ...
People separated from their homes or their loved ones ...
People in the pains of bereavement ...
and to each of them I say:
'May God's abiding company be yours today'
imagining that my prayer may help part the clouds,
and allow the warmth of God's love reach and touch them.

I think of older people who,
with the passing of each day,
must face the reality of approaching death ...
who live within sight of the port up ahead,
and who may be afraid ...
and I pray this blessing:
'May you find the grace to gently let go of life',
imagining that my prayer
may fill their sails,
and encourage them on their final venture.

I think of the young ...
I think of their struggles and their hopes ...
their fears for the future ...
and their cries to be heard, and listened to,
and I pray this blessing:
'May the promise of your youth be met,
may you know love and belonging in your life,
and may your life be fruitful',
and I imagine that the Lord will take my prayer,
my good wishes, and my love,
and keep them safe in his way and in his care.

Finally, I pray for all I will meet today, and I pray:
'May my contact with each person throughout this day
be a special grace for both of us',
and I imagine that the Lord will be there in the meeting,
and that my prayer will be fulfilled.

I come back to my heart now, to rest awhile
in the stillness that I find there ...
and with the sense of worth and goodness,
and with all the loving feelings that have come alive in me
as a result of my prayer for others. Amen.

During the day...

This day is special, it is unique.
It has never before existed, and it will never again return.
It is filled with its own potential,
and is total gift.
Thank you, Lord, for the gift, and for the many blessings
which are wrapped within it.
Thank you, Lord, for entrusting to me something so precious,
something so sacred,
something that is filled with possibilities.
Lord, with this day comes what it takes to live it;

it comes with 'batteries included'
written all over it.
I say my very special Yes that is unique to this day,
and I trust that your Spirit will come upon me,
and the power of the Most High will over-shadow me.
This is the Day of the Lord,
this is the day of salvation.
Incarnation is here, is now, and here am I
right in the midst of it all.

Lead me, Lord, guide my steps, direct my paths.
Make me your touch-person in the lives of others today.
Where there is sadness, let me bring your joy.
Where there is despair, let me bring your hope.
Where there is hatred, let me sow your love.
Melt me, mould me, fill me, use me.
May your Spirit within
touch the hearts of those I meet,
through the prayers I pray,
the words I say,
the life I live,
or the very person that I am.

Today is life.
It is passing, second by second.
It is totally free of yesterday or tomorrow.
'I AM WHO AM' says God,
who is totally a God of NOW.
Please help me drop both arms, Lord:
the one that is trying to change yesterday,
and the one that is trying to arrange tomorrow.
There is only one cross, Lord,
and it is your arms that are outstretched.
You embrace my day,
you embrace my spirit,
and you surround both within the arms of your love.

The gospel is today,
and I am every person in it.
Incarnation is now, and my heart is the manger.
My soul is the Holy Land,
and my inner being is a Pentecost place,
an Upper Room,
a prayer room,
a place where God has made his home.
This is the day that the Lord has made.
Thanks, Lord, for giving me the gift of today,
which is like your down-payment on a day that will never
end.

At night…

There is a time for everything under heaven.
A time to work, and a time to rest,
a time to begin and a time to end,
a time to be born and a time to die.
I took another short step along the road of life today.
I rushed, I crawled, I stopped, I switched off.
The clock continued to move, to count out the seconds,
whether I was moving or not.

I look back on the day, and
I see where I could have done better,
where I missed the moment to say or do the good,
where I drifted, existed, idled, or day-dreamed.
It was a good day, Lord, because you gave it to me.
It was a good day even before it began,
and it still is good, now that it is passing into the room of
the past.

I'm not sure yet just what I learned today,
but it continues to live if it helps make tomorrow better.
Today has been a resume of life,

from the birthing of morning to the dying at night.
Today was your gift,
and you never take back your gifts.
You garner today's harvest, blow away the chaff,
and store the good for the eternal banquets.

I think of people I met today …
Lord, it wasn't easy to see you in some of them!
Please bless them all now, wherever they are.
Remove from their hearts the hurts of today,
and awaken within them the hopes of tomorrow.
I think of those without bed or board tonight …
Of those for whom the nights are long and sleepless …
For those who are terrified of tomorrow …

May my bed be like the palm of your hand.
May I find rest for body, mind, and spirit.
May your Spirit continue to work within me,
bringing to completeness the gestation of incarnation.
Tomorrow will be another day, another life,
requiring another Yes.
Please bless and protect those I love,
and those you have entrusted to me in life,
by way of commitment, responsibility, caring, or ministry.

I finish my day,
as I reach deep within my spirit,
and from there I say a whole-hearted
Thank you, Lord.

15. Thoughts, prayers and whispers

(Short prayers, more by way of thoughts for reflection, than for recitation. It is possible to have a praying heart, to pray all day long, and yet not be 'saying prayers'.)

Lord, I confess to you that I'm not as good as I ought to be, but I thank you that I'm a bit better than I used to be.

****

Lord, please help me accept that everything that happens to me in life can be turned, by you, into a good for my spiritual growth.

****

Lord, I know that you love me exactly as I am, but I believe that you love me much more than that, or you'll leave me the way I am.

****

Lord, I know that you stand at the door and knock, sometimes to enter my heart and at other times to get back out again, through my words and actions.

****

Lord, let there be peace on earth, and let it begin with me.

****

Lord, may your Spirit within me touch the hearts of those I meet today, either through the words I say, the prayers I pray, the life I live, or the very person I am.

****

Lord, I believe that nothing is going to happen today that you and I together will not be able to handle.

****

Lord, you are totally a God of now. Please help me become a person of now, so that I can meet you.

****

Lord, please ensure that, regarding your word, what is mental assent in my head, moves down to become faith in action in my feet.

****

Lord, please remind me that, in the tapestry of life, you see the beauty of the total picture, while I puzzle over the entanglement of threads.

****

Spirit of God, please fill my soul with your power, like helium gas, to give me lift-off out of the quicksand of my own selfishness.

****

Father, you know everything, and I am your child. Please don't let me get so inflated with pride that I know it all, and I try to improve on your knowledge through the intelligence of my conversation, and I call that prayer.

****

Lord, here's one branch that needs to get rid of all of its own sap, if it is to be grafted onto the vine, and draw life from there.

****

Lord, like a harbour pilot, please come out to meet me, take over the helm, and steer me safely into port.

****

Lord, thanks for being with me. At times I discovered that I was in very bad company when I was on my own.

****

The first time I was carried into a church, I was not consulted, and the next time I'll be carried into a church, I won't be consulted either. Lord, I entrust to your care all of the time in between.

****

Lord, if my heart is not praying, my tongue is wasting its

time. Please help me take the cotton wool out of my ears, and put it in my mouth instead.

****

Lord, let me dump all of my past failures into the sea of your love and forgiveness, and to heed the 'No Fishing' sign.

****

Death is like a pile of sand at the end of my life. Lord, please help me sprinkle a little of the sand every day of my life, so that when I reach the end, my dying will already have taken place.

****

Lord, please help me to keep my life within the day, and leave it to you to change yesterday, and to arrange tomorrow.

****

Lord, may your Spirit enter my heart through the cracks of my brokenness.

****

Lord, may my spirit magnify you, so that as you become bigger in my life, my problems will become smaller.

****

Lord, thank you for the gift of life. Please help me have the courage to remove all the wrappings, and to discover the real gift within.

****

Lord, if I am really to be a gift in the lives of others, please help me remove all the price tags.

****

Father, we are all your children. You have no grandchildren, and we all share the inheritance equally. Please help me know my place within your family.

****

Lord, make me a channel of your love and life, rather than a generator or a transformer that controls the flow.

****

Lord, please help me to Come and See, before I attempt to Go and Tell.

****

Lord, let me see my powerlessness as necessary for your victory, and my weaknesses as gateways to knowing your strength.

****

Lord, I sometimes hope that you smile more than cry when you look at us, because we are often more stupid than evil.

****

Lord, please let me know the difference between riches and wealth, between appearance and beauty, between intelligence and wisdom, between achievement and goodwill.

****

Lord Jesus, thank you for telling me that the Father has a big hug waiting for me when I come back to him, even if I have got pig's food all over my face.

****

Lord, please help me to keep things simple, to live one day at a time, and not to attempt to jump the hurdle until I get to it.

****

Spirit of God, I know you understand what I mean when I sometimes think of you as Popeye's spinach.

****

Lord, thank you for living in me, because, as the miles stretch ahead of you, you can see that the things that trip me up are all within me.

****

Lord, please help me to live downstairs in my heart, rather than lock myself away in one of the many rooms within the attic of my mind, where I collect and count my hurts, nurse my resentments, and issue my bills for services rendered.

****

Lord, please open my eyes, my ears, my mind, and my inner being, that I may really enjoy the beauty of your creation all around me.

****

Lord, please give me the patience to continue living with the questions, and the faith to know that the answers will come.

****

Spirit of God, please help me to remember, when everything else fails, that the truth always works.

****

Lord, please keep me close to you and hold me in your love, so that, whether I live or die, our relationship will remain the same.

****

Lord, your message is so simple that it is possible to be too intelligent to understand it, but it is not possible to be too stupid.

****

Lord Jesus, because of what you have done, I believe that the greatest sin I could possibly commit is not to have hope.

****

Lord, please continue to remind me that your kingdom is built among us through the small acts and the hidden efforts.

****

Lord, if you are to mend my brokenness, I know I must let you have all the pieces.

****

Lord, please remind me to turn into a prayer all those things that I turn into a burden.

****